10-6-2

JEANE DIXON'S
ASTROLOGICAL
COOKBOOK

JEANE DIXON'S
ASTROLOGICAL
COOKBOOK

by Jeane Dixon

WILLIAM MORROW AND COMPANY, INC.

NEW YORK   1976

Printed in the United States of America.

1 2 3 4 5 6 7 8 9 10

Library of Congress Cataloging in Publication Data

Dixon, Jeane.
    Jeane Dixon's Astrological cookbook.

    1. Cookery. I. Title. II. Title: Astrological cookbook.
TX652.D56   641.5   76-21798
ISBN 0-688-03091-2

DESIGN   CARL WEISS

THIS BOOK

IS DEDICATED

TO EVERYONE ON THIS FRUITFUL EARTH

WITH THE HOPE THAT,

BY UNDERSTANDING THE FOODS THAT ARE BEST

FOR EACH ONE OF US,

WE MAY USE THEM ALL WISELY

AND SHARE THEM ALL LOVINGLY.

FOREWORD

by Helen Dorsey, M.D.

A large percentage of our supposedly best-fed population complains of chronic malaise and fatigue.

Our young people have the worst eating habits of any generation to date despite the emphasis placed on developing good eating habits by private physicians, clinics, schools, through periodicals and the news media. Junk eating has become almost addictive and nutritious diets are passé. This cannot only lead to terrible acne problems, but does not provide appropriate nutrition for the body to burn, which often leads to disturbing the whole metabolism.

Erratic eating habits pertain to older people as well. Too often they neglect to eat or they subsist on inadequate meals. Working adults who live alone often eat haphazardly. They complain they are too tired to cook at the day's end, can't be bothered cooking for one, or dislike the dishwashing chores. So it behooves us to reevaluate our dietary habits and return young and old alike to the regimens of healthful eating. Strangely enough, the sky-high cost of food today may drive us back to better eating habits!

Careful meal planning is of the utmost importance and implies an elementary knowledge of nutrition. There's hardly any excuse not to eat healthfully today. Many hospitals are staffed with trained dietitians who, by individual appointment, will dispense free advice. There are a number of excellent, inexpensive books on elementary nutrition you can buy, and up-to-date nutrition books can be obtained from your local library.

Choose your diet carefully. Use the commonsense approach! Above all, your diet must be well balanced. There are many good diet plans available. Your doctor will be happy to suggest one. Monumental emphasis must be placed on providing a diet high in protein. Protein-rich eggs, dairy products, legumes, poultry, and particularly fish are excellent, less expensive sources compared to high-priced meats.

Eat fewer carbohydrates and fats, preferably choosing the polyunsaturated fats. If you have a high-cholesterol problem, avoid eating too many eggs. Use a liquid or dried egg substitute.

Generally I suggest a good vitamin supplement for the young or old. For people in their middle years, I suggest a good multiple vitamin only if they have a problem of absorption. Otherwise, you can get your minerals and vitamins from your food.

Avoid food fads. Eating natural foods as we did years ago, before the craze of organic foods, is fine, but not if it's carried to extremes. For example, I've never been one to gather weeds along the wayside. Many of the "health" or organically grown vegetables are the biggest rip off on the market.

Fortunately, backyard gardening is popular once again, making delicious fresh vegetables and fruits readily available at much less cost. These nutritious homegrown bounties are much cheaper than those found in markets, usually excel in flavor and freshness, and are there for the picking.

Variety is extremely important in planning menus, particularly for the obesity or specialty diet. For example, eating cottage cheese for lunch every day is so dull that you'll break the diet out of sheer boredom. Never embark on any strenuous obesity diet without consulting your physcian; a four- or five-pound weight loss is negligible, but seek his advice for greater weight loss. Never skip meals. You're apt to gorge when you're ravenous. Drink lots of water to help you feel full. Never hover over the sink or kitchen counter to eat a meal. In your eyes, you'll consider that snacking instead of eating. Eat in pleasant surroundings.

The biggest challenge of all to the meal planner is in the shopping. You must market very carefully and scrutinize all the labels so you know what you're paying for. Know your brands. Some brands are misleading, and many so-called "diet" or low-calorie foods aren't nearly as low-calorie as they would appear. For example, low-calorie yogurt may in fact be made with yogurt that is low in calories, but fruit that has been sweetened with sugar is added. So you must read labels not only in terms of what you're getting for your money but also for contents.

Cooking and eating can be fun. You should *make* it fun. Since it's something we have to do, we might as well have a good time doing it!

Get your friends and family members to join you in the kitchen. How food looks, how it's served, and atmosphere have a lot to do with the success of your cooking. You don't have to dine by candlelight every night to enjoy your dinner. But even if you're serving only one, it should be a well-cooked, attractively prepared meal. Spices and herbs can help you perk up old family recipes and cut down on salt. You can go that same route by learning to cook food in bouillon instead of salt pork. True, bouillon has some salt in it, but not nearly as much as salt pork or bacon.

Jeane Dixon's Astrological Cookbook provides many interesting and healthful recipes and diversified menus to please almost every palate. Mrs. Dixon also dispenses entertaining astrological culinary comments plus mythological interpretations and folklore associated with food. So, if astrology is your bag, you will find out not only *who* you are but what foods help to make you *what* you are! Even if things celestial fail to charm you, the recipes and menus so capably selected by Mrs. Dixon will turn you on to sound, nutritional meals, both formal and informal, that afford great variety and palatability.

> *Dr. Helen Dorsey, who comes from a family of distinguished physicians and surgeons dating back six generations, has practiced medicine in Hampton, Virginia, for more than thirty years and was the first woman and youngest doctor to serve as chief of staff of Dixie Hospital, one of the state's largest hospitals serving the Tidewater Virginia area.*

CONTENTS

THE ASTROLOGICAL FOODS

Based on Governing Astral Body for Each Decan

Mars: Aries, Libra, Cancer, Scorpio

cayenne	pepper	nettles
garlic	rhubarb	mustard
thistle	onion	radishes
hops	chives	basil
hyssop	leeks	
parsley (also found in Mercury)†	wild lettuce	

Sun: Cancer, Aries, Leo

angelica	lemon
sunflower seeds	lotus
bay leaf	poppy seeds
chamomile (tea)	nutmeg
rosemary	cinnamon
saffron (under Saturn)†	oranges (also under Jupiter)†
walnuts	rice

†Astrological foods sometimes appear under more than one decan, based on herbalists and mythology.

Jupiter: Leo, Cancer, Sagittarius, Aquarius

♃

chervil	asparagus	sage
chestnut (tree)	currants	lime
rose hip	dandelion	
mushrooms	endive	
violet	jasmine tea	
peas	orange (note: included also under sun)†	

Saturn: Capricorn, Taurus, Virgo, Sagittarius

♄

beets	quince
saffron (also under the sun)†	holly
	barley
bistort	
hyssop	

Moon: Cancer, Pisces, Gemini

☽

watercress	cucumbers	cabbage
turnips (also under Mercury)†	melons	zucchini, squash
juniper	pumpkin	lettuce

Neptune: Pisces, Scorpio, Aquarius

♆

pine nuts	lavender

---

†Astrological foods sometimes appear under more than one decan, based on herbalists and mythology.

Venus: Capricorn, Cancer, Virgo, Libra, Aries, Taurus,
♀   Gemini

licorice	thyme	chick-peas
wheat	chestnuts	lentils
sorrel	apple	peaches
plums (prunes)	beans	apricots
plantains	raspberries	blueberries
catnip	pears	cherries
mint	grapes	strawberries

Mercury: Taurus, Sagittarius, Gemini, Aquarius, Leo,
☿   Virgo

carrots	marjoram	parsnips
caraway	savory	mulberry
fennel	pomegranate	hazelnuts
parsley (also	dill	turnips (also
under Mars)†	tea	under the
horehound		moon)†
		fenugreek

Uranus: Libra, Capricorn, Aquarius
♅

contains no astrological foods, but food patterns
determined by psyche

---

†Astrological foods sometimes appear under more than one decan, based on herbalists
and mythology.

INTRODUCTION

HARDLY ANYONE IS AWARE of the importance of selecting foods astrologically—the foods suited to your Zodiac sign—and their harmonizing effect upon your psyche and body.

I'm a strong believer in eating what suits me personally. I feel I must eat foods that are in concert with both my temperament and my body chemistry to fulfill my potential in life. So, quite naturally, that's precisely how I run my kitchen. I'm blessed with psychic powers, but I have learned through the years that if I eat certain foods—namely coffee, tea, chocolate, or quantities of meat—I lose some of my powers of concentration.

I'm a typical Capricorn, born on January 5. Since I'm born under the sign of the goat, dominated by Saturn, I've always been an earth-bound creature, with the tips of my fingers in the heavens, but practical and energetic with plenty of drive. I also fall under the influence of Venus, which stresses the qualities of beauty, harmony, love, cheerfulness, emotion, and introspection. That's why many times I appear withdrawn when I'm not. In reality, I love people and enjoy nothing better than having my family and friends in for a lovely sit-down dinner at home.

My food tastes are simple. Actually, I have the tastes of a

peasant. I adore fresh fruits and garden-grown vegetables. I grew up on frugal German fare, well cooked and beautifully served. I still hanker for the glorious red cabbage and apple küchen I loved as a child. I can still remember the wondrous aroma of German coffee cake baking in the oven wafting through the kitchen making me, oh so hungry!

I've never been keen about meat but I like fish, especially in summer. Fish is light, nutritious, and rich in body-building protein. I'm very fussy about how vegetables should look on the plate. They should not only have eye appeal, but complement each other in flavor and color. I like nothing better than a bouquet of fresh garden vegetables, barely cooked.

I must eat wisely, because I've always enjoyed good health—probably because of my mother. She knew nothing about vitamins, yet she always served interesting, well-balanced meals. I believe in eating my vitamins the natural way. I rely on the same foods my mother used: whole-grain cereals; breads made from unbleached flour; steamed or lightly cooked vegetables; meat, when and if I eat it, I prefer baked, broiled, or braised; generous amounts of dairy products. Typically, I sweeten everything—from jams to marinades—with honey.

Now I'd like to share my feelings about food with you. Cooking astrologically is easy and fun. In this book, I will tell you how astrology can help you know more about yourself and how it relates to your food, your health, and your psyche. You, too, will be able to plan and prepare your own astrological menus. To personalize your menus, each sign is broken down into three decans, each period lasting about ten days.

I'll tell you what astrological foods to choose for each sign. Astrological foods for each decan are marked with an asterisk (*), whether they appear in recipes or in the text copy. All foods are associated with the Zodiac because the cosmic rays—the sun, for example—give life to plants and animals. Plants have to have them in order to grow, even mushrooms that grow in caves.

For centuries man has tried to unlock the mysteries of nature, attributing the change of seasons, ocean tides, and harvest to the cosmic forces. Early astrologers related food to the heavens, believing that astral movements were in some way related to the earthly phenomena that ruled farming, health, and the social order. Many of their beliefs are still found in almanacs. There's a time for planting and a time for harvesting. You have only to consult the almanac to find this kind of advice. For example, one well-known almanac advises the farmer to plant potatoes by the light of the full moon. Herbalists like Culpeper worked out exact times when plants and herbs, governed by the cosmic forces, should be harvested.

Now I've taken away the mystery and will tell you what astrological foods to use for each decan. Special recipes for each decan are designed to include most of the astrological foods to suit the cook's psyche. You can cook for your sign or for the sign of one of your loved ones. For example, as I'm a Capricorn, my astrological foods for this sign are beets, saffron, quince, and barley since my governing planet is Saturn. My birthday falls during the second decan governed by Venus, so I can add on a carload of interesting foods including licorice, wheat, sorrel, plums, plantains, catnip, mint, thyme, chestnuts, apple, beans, raspberries, pears, grapes, chick-peas, and lentils! Tell your loved ones why the meal you've prepared is astrologically sound for them!

The menus have been tailored for virtually every occasion from gala holiday dinners on down; others for quick-off-the-shelf, designed to give the cook new ideas, timely tips, shortcuts, and new ways to prepare old favorites. Allowance is made for both the gourmet and the novice cook.

Above all, menus are simple, designed to keep you in concert with the heartbeat of the universe yet in tune with your psyche and body so you can fulfill your potential in life.

For your interest, I've included some of the folklore, mythology, and astrology along the way. My greatest rewards are the happy at-home dinners with my husband, Jimmy. I experience a warm communal feeling when I break bread with friends and family.

Happy eating!

JEANE DIXON'S
ASTROLOGICAL
COOKBOOK

ARIES: MARCH 21 to APRIL 19

Some Like It Hot!

RULED BY MARS, you are truly a ball of fire! You are impetuous even though you display an outer calm. There's very little mystery about you. You like to lay your cards on the table and tell people exactly what you think!

You are dynamic in the kitchen but hate to linger there. You have a terrific talent for creating quick treats using shortcuts, prepared foods, and your blender. Due to your Martian influences, you favor hot seasonings, onions,* and leeks * in strong-flavored dishes such as chili or tacos and use condiments like mustard * and horseradish.*

Eat meat in moderation—any kind will do. Since you have a low tolerance for stimulants of any kind, abstain or limit alcoholic beverages when you're the cook! You get along best with other "fire people," especially when you entertain on Tuesday at home where you are more comfortable than when you dine out. You like to flank the buffet table with savories, delicious salads, entrées, and rich desserts!

Do all your preparation in advance because you like to sit and talk to your guests. Relax when you can so you won't suffer from headaches and insomnia.

FIRST DECAN: MARCH 21 to MARCH 30

Since you were born under Mars, you are industrious, courageous, and adventuresome in the kitchen. But since you are often impatient, watch out for accidents. In your haste you can burn or cut yourself.

Your menus are easy to execute, interesting, colorful, and different. Due to your dominating nature, you should create informal situations to actively involve your weekend guests in food entertainment. Make-your-own soup is a delightful prelude to dinner and a terrific way to break the ice when you entertain!

ARIEAN SOUP BREAK !* †

Hot Bread Sticks *   Real Raw Fooder Tray *

Vegetable Dunkin' Dip*

Strawberry Creme Mold * or cold Rhubarb, Home Style *

- or -

IMPROMPTU BUFFET

Avocado Butter *   Sour Dough Bread

Chicken Breasts Ratatouille *

---

† The use of an asterisk (*) in menus for each decan indicates 1) that a recipe for the dish is included in the decan, and 2) that the recipe contains one or more astrological foods.

Sliced Tomatoes Vinaigrette

Baked Ham

Corn on the Cob with Cayenne Butter

Ambrosia *

ARIEAN SOUP BREAK

1 can (10¾ oz.) condensed   *¼ tsp. basil leaves,*
    tomato soup   *crushed*
1 soup can water   *yogurt or dairy sour cream*

Heat all ingredients except yogurt or sour cream in small saucepan, stirring constantly. Spoon into cups. Garnish with dollop of yogurt or sour cream. Serves 2.

NOTE: This Ariean sipper can be the beginning of a whole series of different herbs to match your sign or those of your guests! It's a good way to break the ice, particularly with weekend house guests! Aries, Libra, Cancer, and Scorpio: substitute for the basil ¼ to ½ tsp. rosemary * or 1 small clove garlic,* minced. Garnish with chopped chives * or cayenne.* Cancer, Aries, and Leo: substitute 1 small bay leaf * for basil. Garnish with small pieces of lemon peel,* sunflower * or poppy seeds.* Leo, Cancer, Sagittarius, and Aquarius: substitute chervil * for basil. Garnish with slivered fresh mushrooms. Taurus, Capricorn, Virgo, and Sagittarius: Cooked, leftover barley.* For Uranus, and Pisces, great cooks, other touches: *Garnishes:* Use popcorn, corn curls, slivered radishes, or water chestnuts. *Seasonings:* Substitute dill leaves, curry powder, poultry seasoning, or ground sage for basil. *Soups:* For dieters, use condensed chicken or beef soup or tomato soup. Garnish with celery stick, green pepper, or shredded lettuce.

HOT BREAD STICKS

1 pkg. (13¾ oz.) hot roll   ½ tsp. rosemary or oregano
    mix   6 tbsps. butter, melted
1 tbsp. poppy seeds

Prepare dough according to box instructions. Add poppy seed, rosemary (or oregano) to dry ingredients. Cover, let stand in warm place until double in bulk. Divide dough in half. Roll out half on lightly floured (unbleached flour) board to form rectangle 10 × 6 inches, ½ inch thick. Cut into ½-inch strips. Repeat. Place sticks on greased baking sheet. Brush with melted butter. Cover, let double in bulk. Bake in preheated 400° F. oven 10 minutes or until golden for soft texture; 5 minutes longer for crisp brown sticks. Makes 3 dozen sticks.

VEGETABLE DUNKIN' DIP

1½ cups dairy sour cream   few drops Tabasco to taste
½ cup chili sauce
1 tsp. prepared
    horseradish * or
    prepared yellow
    mustard *

Combine all ingredients. Put in small bowl. Refrigerate until ready to use. Makes 2 cups.

REAL RAW FOODER TRAY

carrot sticks
*radishes ***
*red pepper rings ***
cauliflowerets
cherry tomatoes

celery sticks
mushrooms, fresh,
  squeezed with
  few drops lemon juice
green and black olives
Vegetable Dunkin' Dip

Prepare vegetables; refrigerate until ready to use. Arrange on glass or wooden tray with dunkin' sauce in small bowl in center of platter.

STRAWBERRY CREME MOLD

2 envelopes unflavored
   gelatin
⅓ cup honey
⅓ cup cold water
1 can (1 lb. 4 oz.) crushed
   pineapple, undrained
⅔ cup fresh orange juice

⅓ cup fresh lemon juice
2 cups dairy sour cream
2 cups frozen sliced
   strawberries
   or blueberries, thawed
½ cup chopped pecans

Combine gelatin, honey, and water. Cook over low heat, stirring constantly, until gelatin is dissolved. Stir in pineapple with syrup, orange, and lemon juices. Chill until partially set. Fold in sour cream, then fruits and nuts. Fill a 7-cup salad mold; chill until set. Serves 8 to 10.

RHUBARB, HOME STYLE

2 cups 2-inch pieces
   rhubarb *
¼ to ½ cup honey
1 tbsp. margarine

few drops pure vanilla
   extract to taste
sweetened whipped
   cream, optional

Select only tender pink or red rhubarb stalks fresh from the garden. Place cut rhubarb in saucepan. Cover, heat slowly until juice is rendered. Cook uncovered rapidly until rhubarb is almost tender. Stir in honey, simmer until tender (about 30 minutes in all). Remove from heat, add margarine and vanilla. Mix well. Chill well (best left in refrigerator overnight) before serving. Top with whipped cream. Serves 4 to 6.

NOTE: Tart and delicious, rhubarb is fabulous served with roasts or fowl. Delightful mixed with fresh strawberries and bananas or baked in pie with fresh strawberries.

AVOCADO BUTTER

1 mashed California *avocado*	*½ tsp. garlic * salt* *3 dashes Tabasco sauce*

Blend all ingredients. Serve as a spread over sour dough French bread. Lightly broil if desired. Wonderful with vegetarian spaghetti. Makes ¾ cup.

CHICKEN BREASTS RATATOUILLE

3 whole broiler-fryer *chicken breasts, cut in* *half*	*2 small cans okra, drained* *or 1 pkg. frozen okra,* *thawed*
2 tsps. sea salt	*3 tomatoes, peeled and cut*
¼ cup margarine	*in wedges*
1 medium onion,* chopped	*¼ tsp. freshly ground black*
1 clove garlic,* minced	*pepper*
1 green pepper,* cut in *strips*	*¼ tsp. dried rosemary* *1 tsp. chopped parsley**
1 eggplant, cut in ½-inch *slices*	

Sprinkle chicken with salt. Melt margarine; add chicken. Brown on both sides; remove. Add onion, garlic, and green pepper to skillet; cook until tender but not brown; remove. Brown eggplant slices in skillet a few at a time. Add okra and tomatoes to skillet; cook rapidly until tomatoes have cooked down and part of liquid has evaporated. Add cooked onion, garlic, and green pepper with pepper, rosemary, and parsley. Mix well; turn half of mixture into 4-quart casserole. Arrange chicken breasts over vegetables. Place remaining ingredients around chicken. Bake uncovered in 375° F. oven 45 minutes, until chicken is tender. Baste occasionally with liquid from vegetables. Serves 6.

AFTERTHOUGHTS: Can be made in advance and baked just

before serving. Add grated Romano or Parmesan cheese over top to form crust (run under broiler to brown) to make a hearty main dish.

AMBROSIA

6 oranges*
honey
2 bananas
1 cut lemon

1 can water-packed
   pineapple chunks,
   drained
shredded coconut

Peel, dice oranges; sweeten with honey. Peel bananas; cut in large pieces. Squeeze with fresh lemon to keep banana from turning brown. Combine banana and pineapple chunks with sweetened oranges. Spoon into glass serving dishes. Garnish with coconut. Serve very cold. Serves 4 to 6.

SECOND DECAN: MARCH 31 to APRIL 10

Add the qualities of the sun and you really shine in the kitchen! Your ambitious ways make you more interested in food as entertainment than simply lingering over a hot stove.

You adore being with people. What better way to see them than to feed them one of your terrific buffets! With your innate talent for quick fix-ups, you can whisk up a colorful, delicious, eye-appealing menu in jig time. Leftovers or quick treats off the emergency shelf are a challenge. Your sunny astrological foods include rice,* rosemary,* walnuts,* lemon,* poppy seeds,* and oranges.*

ARIEAN STYLE CHILI *

Hot Macaroni Salad *   Lazy Susan Salad *

Assorted Cold Cuts   Tuna Fish Salad

Bacon Chive Corn Muffins * or Poppy Seed * Rolls

Fresh Fruit Tray   Assorted Cheeses

Coffee   Tea

ARIEAN STYLE CHILI

2 lbs. ground beef
1 tbsp. vegetable oil
1 can (15 oz.) tomato sauce
1 can (1 lb.) kidney beans,
   undrained

1½ tbsps. instant minced
   onion
2 tsps. chili powder
1 bay leaf*
2 cups shredded Cheddar
   cheese

Brown meat in large skillet. Stir in tomato sauce, beans, onion, chili powder, and bay leaf. Bring to boil; simmer 30 minutes. Remove bay leaf. Remove from heat; stir in cheese until melted. Garnish each serving with additional Cheddar cheese. Serves 4.

NOTE: Aromatic with onion, hearty but fast-paced, well geared to suit the Ariean cook. Better double or triple recipe for a crowd. You can always freeze remainder.

HOT MACARONI SALAD

2 tbsps. chopped onion
⅛ tsp. caraway or poppy
   seed*
2 tbsps. butter or
   margarine

1 can (14¾ oz.) macaroni
   and cheese
½ cup cooked sliced carrots
½ cup cooked, cut string
   beans

In saucepan, cook onion with caraway or poppy seed in butter until tender. Add remaining ingredients. Heat; stir occasionally. Serves 4.

NOTE: Double or triple recipe for a crowd. Zip up tanginess by adding prepared mustard or horseradish to taste.

LAZY SUSAN SALAD

2 heads western iceberg
  lettuce
1 cup dairy sour cream
½ cup mayonnaise
2 tbsps. lemon * juice
1 tsp. dry mustard
½ tsp. sea salt
¼ tsp. onion powder

3 cups cooked vegetables
  (beans, cauliflower,
  carrots, or corn)
  marinated in corn oil,
  vinegar, and
  seasonings to taste
1 cup red onion rings
1 pint cottage cheese
2 cups julienne cooked
  ham

Core, rinse, and drain lettuce. Chill in disposable bags until ready to use. Just before serving, blend sour cream with mayonnaise, lemon juice, mustard, salt, and onion powder. Place in bowl in center of large round platter. Cut lettuce into wedges, approximately 4 per head; arrange alternately with marinated vegetables, onion rings, cheese, and ham around edge of platter. Serves 8.

BACON CHIVE CORN MUFFINS

1 pkg. (12 oz.) corn
  muffin mix
2 tsps. dried chives
  dash freshly ground
  black pepper

1 egg
⅔ cup milk
½ cup crisp crumbled
  bacon

Combine corn muffin mix, dried chives, and pepper in mixing bowl. Continue muffin preparation, adding egg and milk according to package directions. Fold in crumbled bacon. Turn into 12 greased 2¾-inch muffin tins lined with paper liners. Bake in preheated 400° F. oven 20 to 25 minutes or until done. Serve hot. Makes 12 muffins.

THIRD DECAN: APRIL 11 to APRIL 19

Aries are sociable, romantic, more in tune with themselves than most. However, you are sometimes a bit erratic. One minute you are compassionate and artistic; the next minute, lazy but tidy!

You're a stand-out in a supermarket crowd where you always indulge your special tastes: fresh fruits (apples,* strawberries,* pears,* peaches,* plums, * and grapes *) and vegetables.

Because you're romantic, you like to decorate your table with spring flowers. If you don't have a garden, you make a dash for the flower peddler, especially when you're dining with the love of your life. You are happiest around other fire people like yourself—Sagittarians or Leonians.

You like an easy menu that you can cook by remote control in a Dutch oven or a crock pot!

PLANETARY OLD-FASHIONED POT ROAST *

Waldorf Salad (celery, apples,* grapes *)

Rosy Posy Pears *

Orange Tea

- or -

HUNGARIAN VEGETABLE GOULASH *

Buttered Noodles

Lettuce, Radish, Red Pepper Salad

Snow Pudding with Lemon
Custard Sauce

PLANETARY OLD-FASHIONED POT ROAST

2 cans (10½ oz.) condensed
  beef broth
1 boneless pot roast,
  weighing 3 or 4 lbs.
2 tbsps. vegetable oil
1 tsp. original
  Worcestershire
  sauce
½ tsp. sea salt

⅛ tsp. freshly ground
  pepper
1 bay leaf
6 large carrots, peeled, cut
  in 2-inch pieces
4 medium potatoes, peeled,
  cut in half
⅓ cup unbleached flour,
  optional

Reserve ¾ cup broth; set aside. Brown roast in vegetable oil in Dutch oven; pour off fat. Add remaining broth, Worcestershire, salt, pepper, and bay leaf. Cover, cook slowly 1½ hours. Add carrots and potatoes; cook 45 minutes longer or until vegetables are tender. Gradually blend reserved broth with flour until smooth; slowly stir into sauce. Cook, stir until thickened. Taste to correct seasonings. Serve roast on warm platter surrounded by vegetables. Pass sauce in gravy boat. Serves 6 to 8.

AFTERTHOUGHTS: For dieters, skip the flour. Add all the broth at the beginning. Cook as directed; add more liquid (water or diluted broth) as needed. During last hour, remove lid, allowing broth to evaporate. Serve roast with natural juices. Prepared horseradish is a terrific condiment to serve with beef!

ROSY POSY PEARS *

3 *fresh California Bartlett
pears* *
2 *cups fresh strawberries* *

1½ *cups fresh blueberries or
1 pkg. (10 oz.) frozen
blueberries,* *
thawed and drained*
½ *cup red currant jelly*
½ *cup rosé wine*

Pare, halve, and core pears; cut lengthwise into slices. Cut strawberries lengthwise into halves. Combine pears and berries in shallow bowl. Melt jelly over low heat; stir in wine. Pour sauce over fruit, tossing occasionally. Serves 6 to 8.

HUNGARIAN VEGETABLE GOULASH

2 *lbs. lean round steak, cut
in 2-inch cubes*
1 *large onion, chopped*
1 *clove garlic, pressed*
1 *tsp. sea salt*
¼ *tsp. lemon pepper*
½ *tsp. rosemary*
1 *tbsp. paprika*
1 *tbsp. original
Worcestershire sauce*

1 *large bay leaf, crushed*
4 *large tomatoes, peeled,
chopped*
4 *potatoes, scrubbed, cut in
large pieces*
4 *carrots, scrubbed, diced*
6 *or 8 pearl onions, peeled*
1 *cup green beans,* *frozen*
1 *cup dairy sour cream*

Put beef, onion, and garlic in crock pot. Combine salt, lemon, pepper, rosemary, and paprika; sprinkle over meat. Add ½ cup water and all remaining ingredients except sour cream. Cover, cook about 8 hours. Stir in sour cream 5 minutes before serving. Serve alone or over noodles as desired. Serves 6.

TAURUS: APRIL 20 to MAY 20

A Matter of Taste!

YOU ARE GENERALLY cautious, shrewd, steadfast, but obstinate!
Usually gentle, you're not when you've been crossed. Then you
turn into a bear, lose control, and you're better off left alone.

You want only the good things in life, meaning great but
simple dinners at home or in quiet places. You have that
famous "Taurean taste." For you, that means only the best. If
you can't have the finest steak, fruits, or vegetables, you'd
rather have nothing at all. You like your kitchen beautiful and
functional, your dining room romantic (influenced by Venus,
your ruling planet). Since you have a love for good food and
wine, you have an instinctive ability to cook well. Your greatest
problem is your tendency to overindulge your Taurean taste!

Taurean menus are fun because they include many versatile
but low-calorie foods: wheat,* beans,* chestnuts,* lentils,*
chick-peas,* apples,* strawberries,* raspberries,* pears,*
peaches,* grapes.* Herbs (thyme,* mint,* and catnip *) and
well-seasoned vegetables are special for Taureans. Celery tops
the list of foods to help dieting Taureans.

Friday is your best day for entertaining. Taurus, Capricorn,
and Virgo types turn you on!

FIRST DECAN: APRIL 20 to APRIL 29

Since you are strongly influenced by Venus, you shift from positive to negative, displaying affection, grace, humanity, and refinement or laziness, loudness, and excessive outbursts by turns!

You crave beautiful, traditional dishes of quality, however simple or basic they may be. Taurean women are terrific at baking bread, cakes, pies, and confections. You delight in preserving early summer fruits in chutneys, jams, and conserves using fruit from your garden or tree.

The best fun of all is the coffee break, when you spread homemade bread with your home-produced jam!

VENUSIAN COFFEE BREAK

Homemade Bread *   Apricot Chutney *

Raspberry-Pear Jam *

Fresh Sweet Butter

or African Bread * with Spiced Butter *

Coffee   Hot Spiced Tea

- or -

LEMONY LEG OF LAMB *

Fresh Mint Sauce *   Minted Pears *

Oven-Roasted Potatoes   Carrots

Brussels Sprouts *

Strawberries * in Raspberry* Sauce

HOMEMADE BREAD

1 pkg. dry active yeast   *2 eggs plus 1 white, beaten*
about 3½ cups unbleached   *1 tsp. sea salt*
* flour*   *½ cup warm milk*
¼ cup honey   *⅓ cup melted margarine*
½ cup lukewarm water

Combine yeast, 1 cup flour, honey, and ½ cup water in large mixing bowl. Beat well. Set bowl in pan of warm water. Cover with towel. Let rise in warm place, free from drafts, until doubled in bulk. Add beaten eggs to remaining ingredients. Add egg-flour mixture to yeast sponge, beating hard until dough is smooth and elastic. Put bowl back in warm water. Cover, let dough rise until doubled in bulk. Punch down dough. Roll out dough to form loaf to fit into greased 5- × 10-inch bread pan. Cover, let rise until dough has almost risen to top of pan. Bake in preheated 400° F. oven 15 minutes; reduce oven temperature to 325° F. Bake about 30 minutes longer or until bread is done. Turn out on wire rack to cool. Cover lightly with cloth. Makes 1 loaf.

NOTE: Bread freezes nicely. Make in quantity for coffee break or cold roast lamb sandwiches spread with apricot chutney!

APRICOT * CHUTNEY

¾ *cup California dried
apricots,* finely chopped*
¼ *cup water*
¼ *cup honey*
1 *cup tart apples,* finely
diced*
¼ *cup raisins * or currants*
1 *tbsp. onion, minced*

2 *tbsps. fresh lemon or lime
juice*
¼ *tsp. ground ginger*
¼ *cup packaged, shredded
coconut*
2 *or 3 drops Tabasco*
½ *tsp. lemon or lime rind,
finely grated*

Combine apricots, water, and honey in saucepan; cover and bring to a boil. Reduce heat and simmer for 2 or 3 minutes (or until water is absorbed). Stir frequently; cool. Combine cooled apricots with all remaining ingredients. Let stand at room temperature at least 1 hour before serving. Lovely accompaniment to serve with poultry, lamb, or pork roasts. To store, cover in refrigerator up to a week. Makes about 1½ cups.

RASPBERRY *-PEAR * JAM

6 to 8 fresh California
Bartlett pears *
2 baskets fresh
raspberries *

3 tbsps. fresh lemon or lime
juice
1 pkg. (1¾ oz.) powdered
fruit pectin
3¾ cups sugar

Quarter, core, and finely chop pears; mash on cutting board with fork and pack into measuring cup to get 4 cups. Clean, pick over raspberries, and pack into measuring cup to get 1¼ cups. Combine fruits, lime or lemon juice, and pectin in kettle. Bring to a boil. Boil one minute, stirring, then add sugar. Cook, stirring, until it returns to boil. Boil vigorously one minute. Remove from heat; stir and skim for five minutes to cool slightly and remove foam on top. Pour into hot sterilized jars; seal at once with melted paraffin. Makes about 7 ½-pint jars.

SPICED BUTTER

Combine 1 cup butter or margarine, 1 tsp. onion powder, ½ tsp. turmeric, ¼ tsp. each garlic powder, cardamon, and cinnamon. Heat slowly until bubbling hot. Cool before using.

AFRICAN BREAD WITH SPICED BUTTER

1½ cups warm water	*1 tsp. white pepper*
2 pkgs. active dry yeast	*⅛ tsp. cayenne*
¾ cup spiced butter	*2½ tsps. sea salt*
1 tsp. powdered coriander	*5 to 5½ cups unbleached*
1 tsp. powdered cardamon	*flour*

Rinse bowl with warm water. Add 1½ cups warm water. Sprinkle yeast in water. Let stand until thoroughly moistened. Stir in ¾ cup spiced butter, coriander, cardamon, pepper, cayenne, and salt. Blend in flour, 1 cup at a time, to make a moderately stiff dough. Turn out onto floured board; knead 5 minutes. Pinch off a ball about 1 to 1¼ inches in diameter for center of loaf. Shape remainder into a flat round about 9½ inches in diameter on an ungreased baking sheet. With a sharp knife, make shallow cuts spoke fashion on top. Center with the reserved ball of dough. Brush with more spiced butter. Cover, let rise in warm place until doubled (about 1 to 1½ hours). Bake in preheated 350° F. oven 50 to 60 minutes. Brush again with remaining spiced butter as soon as loaf is removed from oven. Makes 1 large loaf.

LEMONY LEG OF LAMB

1 5-lb. leg of lamb
1 lemon
2 cloves garlic, peeled,
   minced
½ tsp. lemon pepper
1 tsp. sea salt
¼ cup pan drippings
3 tbsps. unbleached flour

2 cups water
freshly ground black pepper
6 small potatoes, scrubbed
1 bunch carrots, scrubbed,
   cut in large pieces
Minted pears,* optional

Place lamb on rack in open shallow roasting pan. Trim only zest (yellow rind) from lemon peel; mince finely. Mix rind with garlic, lemon pepper, and salt. Rub garlic mixture over surface of lamb. Insert meat thermometer in thickest part of lamb but do not let it touch bone. Roast lamb at 300° F. until meat thermometer registers 175° F. (rare). Parboil potatoes and carrots 10 minutes in boiling salted water. Arrange potatoes and carrots around roast during last 1½ hours of roasting time, turning at least 3 times to ensure even browning and cooking. Remove lamb to heated platter. Skim off excess fat; discard. Reserve ¼ cup pan drippings; stir in flour. Cook over low heat, stirring until mixture is thick and smooth. Stir in water, cook over low heat, stirring to desired thickness. Taste to correct seasonings. Pass lamb gravy as side dish to serve over lamb and vegetables. Serve with minted pears * or fresh mint * sauce. Serves 6.

FRESH MINT * SAUCE

⅓ cup chopped fresh mint *
   leaves
½ cup white vinegar

2 tbsps. water
1 tbsp. honey

Heat mint leaves in mixture of vinegar, water, and honey. Simmer, then keep warm 30 minutes, allowing mint to steep 30 minutes before serving with lamb. Makes ¾ cup.

MINTED PEARS *

2 tbsps. fresh mint * or 1½
tsps. dried mint flakes *
2 tbsps. lemon juice
¼ cup honey

4 to 6 pears,* fresh or
canned
2 tbsps. melted butter

Combine mint, lemon juice, and honey. Let stand in warm place while lamb cooks. Cut pears into quarters, place cut sides up in shallow pan. Drizzle with butter, then mint mixture. Broil several inches from heat, 8 to 10 minutes, basting frequently until glazed. Serve warm. Serves 6 to 8.

BRUSSELS SPROUTS

4 cups Brussels sprouts
2 cups cold water
½ cup salt
3 tbsps. butter

3 tbsps. minced onion
¼ cup beef broth
freshly ground black pepper
to taste

Soak sprouts in cold water to which salt has been added. Drain. Cut away thick base where leaves are sparse. Drop few sprouts at a time into 2 quarts rapidly boiling water; cook uncovered about 5 minutes. Taste. If necessary cook 2 minutes longer or until almost tender. Drain. Shake dry over low heat. Melt butter in saucepan. Stir in onion; cook quickly until onion is tender. Add broth and sprouts. Coat sprouts with sauce. Simmer uncovered until liquid has been absorbed and sprouts are completely cooked. Salt and pepper lightly to taste. Serves 6.

STRAWBERRIES * IN RASPBERRY * SAUCE

*1 quart large strawberries **   *3 tbsps. Grand Marnier*
3 cups frozen, thawed   *fresh mint leaves*
  *raspberries **

Rinse, dry, hull, and chill strawberries. Purée raspberries in blender; add Grand Marnier and chill. Several hours before dinner, arrange strawberries on a large glass serving dish. Pour raspberry sauce over strawberries. Chill. Garnish with mint leaves. Serves 6 to 8.

AFTERTHOUGHTS: A perfect example of the Taurean's preference for beautiful food. In later summer, use fresh raspberries. If desired, substitute Framboise liquor for Grand Marnier and sweeten slightly if desired with a minuscule amount of strained honey. Or skip booze and serve "au naturel."

SECOND DECAN: APRIL 30 to MAY 10

Add the qualities of Saturn and you slow down to a halting pace. Your behavior confuses your friends and family because you waver between being industrious, responsible, and happy or cautious, doubtful, and pessimistic!

Don't direct your problems to the table. Exercise great control by staying near friends and family who swing with your moods. Now is the time to exercise that terrific ambition you pick up from Saturn and learn to cut down on calories. Since you have a flare for cooking, learn to prepare meals that work for both you and your nondieting friends.

———

SUPERB LEMON BARBECUED STEAK *

Sweet-Sour Beets (Pickles) *

Taurean Fruit and Celery Salad *

Blueberries or Blueberry Freezer Pie *

- or -

TUNA SALAD, HELEN *

Water Biscuits

Cup of Beef Broth

SUPERB LEMON BARBECUED STEAK

½ tsp. lemon rind, grated
½ cup fresh lemon juice
3 tbsps. fine-grade olive oil
¾ tsp. sea salt
freshly ground black pepper

½ tsp. original
Worcestershire sauce
1 tsp. prepared yellow
mustard
1 chopped green onion,
optional
1½ lbs. boneless sirloin steak

Combine all ingredients except meat. Pour over meat in shallow dish. Let stand 2 hours at room temperature or 4 hours in refrigerator. Turn several times in marinade. Remove from marinade; pat dry. Cook over coals for 7 to 8 minutes, turn and cook 7 to 8 minutes more for medium rare. Brush with marinade occasionally. Serves 4.

NOTE: Can be broiled indoors as well. Like its name, you must buy top-quality steak before you start to barbecue!

SWEET-SOUR BEETS (PICKLES) *

1 cup honey
1⅓ cups water
2 cups vinegar
2 sticks cinnamon, 2 inches long
½ tsp. whole allspice

½ tsp. whole cloves
1½ tsps. sea salt
*6 cups sliced cooked beets **
1 cup sliced raw onion

Combine honey, water, vinegar, and cinnamon in saucepan. Tie together allspice and cloves in small cheesecloth bag; add to vinegar solution. Bring to a boil; simmer 3 minutes. Add salt, beets, and onion. Simmer 5 minutes. Remove spice bag; add cinnamon. Pack in hot sterilized jars. Seal at once. Makes 8 half-pint jars.

NOTE: Terrific to grow and can from your garden. Do not use canned beets for at least six weeks. Eat tender young beet tops barely cooked in water, then drained and served with hot seasoned butter—sensational with smoked pork chops!

TAUREAN FRUIT AND CELERY SALAD

1 can (11 oz.) Mandarin
  oranges
2 apples, skin left on,
  chopped

2 stalks celery, chopped
*½ cup raisins ***
diet salad dressing or
  mayonnaise

Drain oranges; reserve liquid to soak raisins. Prepare other fruits. Drain raisins; combine with oranges, fruits. Toss lightly with small amount of salad dressing. Serves 4.

NOTE: Substitute grapes for raisins for dieters.

BLUEBERRY FREEZER PIE

1 baked 9-inch pie shell
1 pkg. (3 oz.) diet
  strawberry gelatin
1¼ cups boiling water
1 pint vanilla ice cream

2 cups fresh or frozen
  blueberries
1 cup heavy cream,
  whipped
¼ cup confectioners' sugar
1 tsp. pure vanilla extract

Cool pie shell. Dissolve gelatin in boiling water. Cut ice cream into cubes, drop cubes into hot gelatin one at a time, stir until ice cream is melted. Chill until slightly thickened. Fold in 1½ cups of the blueberries. Pour filling into pie shell. Chill until firm. Whip cream with sugar and vanilla. Put cream into pastry bag and pipe with a rosette tip into a lattice on the pie. Fill lattice with remaining blueberries. Chill until ready to serve. Serves 6 to 8.

NOTE: Make diet version of pie using diet cream topping and artificial sweetener.

TUNA SALAD, HELEN

1 head western iceberg
  lettuce
4 cans (3½ oz. or 7 oz.)
  water-pack tuna, drained
2 tbsps. chopped pimiento
1 tsp. fresh lemon juice
1 cup diet mayonnaise
8 strips pimiento

12 carrot curls
8 green onions
8 celery fans
8 ripe olives
4 lemons
parsley sprigs

Core, rinse, and thoroughly drain lettuce; chill in disposable plastic bag or lettuce crisper. Line serving plates with outer lettuce leaves. Place one whole can of tuna atop lettuce on each plate. Combine chopped pimiento and lemon juice with mayonnaise; spoon onto tuna. Decorate with crossed pimiento strips. Garnish plate with carrot, onions, celery, olives, lemon "flower" (cut lemon into wedges not quite through and spread "petals"), and parsley. Makes 4 salads.

NOTE: To make celery "fans," cut celery into pieces about 3 inches long. Make lengthwise cuts about 1½ inches about ⅛ inch apart. Store in cold water until curled into "fans."

THIRD DECAN: MAY 11 to MAY 20

Add the influences of Mercury and you become a pleasure seeker wanting the best in love, food, and drink. It's small wonder that you excel in the kitchen—Escoffier was a Taurean! Since you're a purist at heart, keep the menu simple and forget the sauces.

Lady Taureans often dig the rustic life. Therefore base your menus on bounty from the garden. Taurean men and women both agree, the best of everything must start with a good hunk of meat; then bring on the fruits and vegetables!

DINNER

London Broil Scotty *

Lettuce Casserole Carousel *

Marinated Green Beans *

Nectarine-Strawberry Cup

- or -

LUNCHEON

Taurean Salmon Mold *

Fresh Strawberries   Iced Tea

LONDON BROIL SCOTTY

*1 piece London broil
steak, weighing about 3
lbs.
1 cut lemon
about ½ cup top-quality soy
sauce*

*1 small clove garlic,
pressed
freshly ground black pepper*

Rub steak with cut lemon. Place steak in flat glass or china dish. Pour soy sauce and garlic over steak. Cover, turn several times, and refrigerate 8 hours or even overnight. Broil in very hot oven on both sides to desired degree of doneness. Season well with freshly ground pepper. Serves 4.

NOTE: If desired, you can "gild" the steak by adding a pat of savory butter to steak just before serving! Flavor soft butter with finely chopped savory—fresh is terrific—a few drops fresh lemon or sauterne, a few grains of white pepper, and a *tiny* bit of finely chopped chives. The results are fantastic. The recipe is from a Scottish lady, who, like her sign, believes in eating nothing but the best!

LETTUCE CASSEROLE CAROUSEL

1 head western iceberg
  lettuce
⅓ cup margarine
¼ cup finely chopped onion
½ tsp. crumbled tarragon or
  savory *
¼ tsp. sea salt
⅛ tsp. freshly ground black
  pepper

¼ cup chopped fresh parsley
1 pkg. frozen green peas,
  thawed
1 can (12 oz.) whole kernel
  corn, drained
12 cherry tomatoes or 6
  small tomato halves

Core, rinse, and drain lettuce well; cut into 4 wedges. Combine margarine, onion, tarragon, salt, and pepper in saucepan. Sauté until onion is tender-crisp. Stir in parsley. Heap peas into 2 triangles opposite each other in shallow 10-inch round baking dish. Heap corn into 2 triangles between peas. Place tomatoes around edge and in center. Arrange lettuce wedges cut sides up over peas and corn. Pour butter sauce over all. Cover tightly; bake in preheated 450° F. oven 15 minutes or just until peas are cooked and lettuce is still crisp. Serves 6 to 8.

MARINATED GREEN BEANS

2 pkgs. (9 ozs. each) frozen   1 tsp. honey
   cut green beans   ½ tsp. sea salt
6 tbsps. salad oil   ¼ tsp. freshly ground black
2 tbsps. vinegar   pepper
2 tsps. marjoram leaves,†
   crumbled

Cook beans according to package instructions, only until crisp-tender. Drain, cool. In small bowl, combine oil, vinegar, marjoram, honey, salt, and pepper. Beat until blended. Pour dressing over green beans; cover, marinate in refrigerator 12 hours. Serves 6.

---

† A delightful way to feature marjoram to please the most discerning Taurean palate.

TAUREAN SALMON MOLD

2 envelopes unflavored
gelatin
1 can (12½ oz.) chicken
consommé
1 tbsp. fresh lemon juice
¼ tsp. sea salt
6 hard-cooked eggs
1 can (1 lb.) red salmon
¼ cup salmon liquid
½ cup celery, minced
1 can (3 oz.) mushrooms,
drained and chopped
1 tsp. instant minced onion

¼ cup water
¼ cup vinegar
2 tsps. honey
2 tsps. ground marjoram
1 tsp. parsley flakes
½ tsp. celery salt
¼ tsp. freshly ground black
pepper
½ cup heavy cream,
whipped
cleaned crisp Swiss chard
marinated green beans

Sprinkle 1 envelope of gelatin over ½ cup consommé in saucepan. Cook over low heat, stirring until gelatin is dissolved. Remove from heat; stir in remaining consommé, lemon juice, and salt. Pour into bottom of 6-cup ring mold. Chill until almost firm. Cut eggs in half lengthwise; arrange in gelatin, with yolks face down. Chill until gelatin is firm. Drain salmon and reserve ¼ cup liquid. Remove bones from salmon and flake. Add celery and mushrooms, toss lightly. In saucepan combine reserved salmon liquid and instant onion. Add remaining envelope of gelatin, water, vinegar, honey, marjoram, parsley, celery salt, and pepper. Cook; stir over low heat until gelatin is dissolved. Remove from heat; chill until consistency of unbeaten egg whites. Mix gelatin thoroughly with flaked salmon mixture. Fold in whipped cream. Spoon lightly over eggs in ring mold; spread evenly with spatula. Chill until firm. Unmold on bed of Swiss chard on serving plate. Fill center with marinated green beans. Serves 6.

GEMINI: MAY 21 to JUNE 20

Offbeat Palate!

YOU'RE BETTER KNOWN for being erratic than for your ability to cook, due to your constantly shifting Mercurial nature. You owe your dual personality to your sign, the twins! That's why you burn up tremendous energy and rely on mini-meals, appetizers, and nourishing and quick, light treats. Food must be offbeat, exciting.

Your curiosity about life makes you terrific fun to be around. You literally turn people on to food just by the way you talk about your travels—dining in distant bistros or sampling strange new taste treats. Your only hangup is indecision! It's tough to know what and when to serve at home. Since you are often a vegetarian, you thrive on a diet of fruits * and nuts.* Load up on milk plus green foods and carrot combinations. You need a summery food supply like the season which marks your rise in the heavens. Nuts, fruits, vegetables, melons in salads or repasts suit your offbeat palate. You particularly love to dine with Aries, Leo, Libra, and Aquarius types!

Normally you are jet-propelled and a night person. Often you're an insomniac and need plenty of sleep to quiet your sometimes jangled nerves.

FIRST DECAN: MAY 21 to MAY 30

Since you are ruled by Mercury, you are a speed demon in the kitchen. You have excellent hand dexterity and can do two things at once—like talking on the phone while emptying the dish washer, or ironing a shirt while listening to your kids go over their multiplication tables.

You can talk your friends into eating almost anything. In fact, your enthusiasm makes them remember what you said more than what you prepared!

Often you're plagued by indecision. Plan a menu for early- as well as for late-night noshing, starring your favorite Geminian creations!

SEASONED POPCORN *

Carrot-Nut Salad *   Olive Dilled Salad *

Stuffed Vegetarian Eggplant *

Mini Hot Dogs in Tiny Buns   Bran Health Bread * and Butter

Strawberries 'n Cream Cake *

- or -

BASIC BAGEL *

Bagel Lunch/Brunch *

with all the fixings

California Caesar Salad *   Carrots 'n Grapes *

Strawberries Sublime (whipped cream
or yogurt, ground cinnamon*
or ground mace, honey)

Coffee   Tea   Sangria

SEASONED POPCORN

For seasoning:
  6 *tbsps. sea salt*
  2 *tsps. paprika*
  1 *tsp. dry mustard*

½ *tsp. each: garlic salt,*
celery salt, thyme,
marjoram,* curry
powder, and dill weed *

Combine all ingredients. Store in covered jar. Make ½ cup.

For popcorn:
  3 *qts. unsalted popped*
  popcorn

½ *cup melted butter*
3 *tbsps. seasoning*

Heat popcorn in 250° F. oven if it has been popped earlier.
Pour butter over popcorn, tossing to mix. Sprinkle with
seasonings; toss until well blended. Makes enough for a "small
army." It really tastes like "More!"

NOTE: 1 oz. unpopped popcorn kernels (2 tbsps. household
measure) makes about 1 qt. popped corn.

OLIVE DILLED * SALAD

1 pkg. (9 oz.) frozen
artichoke hearts
1 cup boiling water
1 head romaine lettuce,
torn into bite-size pieces
1 cup watercress
1 cup small whole
pimiento-stuffed olives
½ cup olive oil

¼ cup wine vinegar
4 tsps. fresh dill,* chopped
1 tbsp. fresh parsley,*
chopped
1½ tsps. honey
1 tsp. Dijon mustard
1 tsp. sea salt
¼ tsp. freshly ground black
pepper

Plunge artichoke hearts in boiling water; remove pan from heat. Let stand few minutes. Drain, chill in large salad bowl. Combine artichoke hearts, romaine, watercress, and olives. In small jar with tight-fitting lid, combine olive oil, vinegar, dill, parsley, honey, mustard, salt, and pepper. Shake well. Just before serving, pour dressing over salad. Toss to coat well. Serves 6 to 8.

STUFFED VEGETARIAN EGGPLANT

1 *large eggplant weighing*
   2 lbs.
1 *cup chopped green*
   pepper
½ *cup chopped onion*
¼ *cup butter*
1 *can (1 lb.) tomatoes,*
   drained

1 *cup shredded Swiss*
   cheese
½ *cup chopped dry roasted*
   peanuts
1 *tsp. basil, crushed*
½ *tsp. sea salt*
⅛ *tsp. freshly ground black*
   pepper

Cut slice from across top of eggplant. Cut around inside edge of eggplant keeping ½ inch from edge. Scoop out center, leaving ½-inch shell. Partially cook shell in boiled salted water; drain. Cube eggplant meat; partially cook in boiling salted water 5 minutes; drain. Sauté cubed eggplant, green pepper, and onion in butter until tender. Add remaining ingredients; spoon into eggplant shell. Place in greased shallow baking dish. Cover. Bake in preheated 350° F. oven 30 minutes or until tender. Serves 6 to 8.

BRAN HEALTH BREAD

4½ to 5½ cups unsifted
  unbleached flour
2 tbsps. raw sugar
2 tsps. sea salt
2 pkgs. active dry yeast
2 cups whole bran cereal

1 cup milk
½ cup water
2 tbsps. honey or dark
  molasses
⅓ cup butter or margarine
2 eggs

Mix together 1 cup flour, sugar, salt, and undissolved yeast in large mixing bowl. Add cereal. Combine milk, water, honey (or molasses), and butter (or margarine) in saucepan. Heat until warm but butter is not melted. Gradually add dry ingredients, beat 2 minutes at medium speed, using electric mixer, scraping bowl occasionally. Add eggs and ½ cup flour (enough to make a thick batter). Beat at high speed 2 minutes, scraping bowl occasionally. Stir in enough additional flour to make a soft dough. Turn out onto lightly floured board. Knead until dough is smooth and elastic. Place in greased bowl, turn to grease top. Cover; let rise in warm place, free from drafts, until doubled in bulk. Punch down dough. Turn out onto lightly floured board. Divide dough in 2 equal parts. Shape dough into 2 loaves. Place in well-greased 8½- × 4½-inch loaf pans. Cover. Let rise in warm place, free from drafts, until doubled in bulk (about 1 hour). Bake in lowest rack position in preheated 375° F. oven 35 minutes or until bread sounds hollow when thumped on side with the fingers. Remove from pans. Grease tops. Cool on wire racks. Makes 2 loaves.

STRAWBERRIES 'N CREAM CAKE

*1 pkg. (14½ oz.) angel food
    cake mix
2 pts. fresh strawberries
3 tbsps. honey*

*1 pt. heavy cream
¼ cup sugar
1 tsp. lemon peel, grated
2 tsps. vanilla extract*

Prepare cake according to package instructions using either an ungreased 15- × 4-inch loaf pan or a 10-inch tube pan. Cool cake. Cover, store overnight for easier slicing. Next day, set aside ½ cup strawberries for garnish. Slice remaining strawberries, add honey to taste. Slice cake crosswise into 3 even layers. Whip cream with ¼ cup sugar, lemon peel, and vanilla until soft peaks form. Spread ⅓ of whipped cream on bottom cake layer; cover with ½ of sliced strawberries. Add second cake layer and repeat procedure. Add top cake layer; spread with remaining whipped cream. Garnish cake with reserved whole strawberries. Chill several hours. Slice cake with serrated knife. Serves 12.

BASIC BAGEL

1½ cups warm water
1 pkg. active dry yeast or
  1 cake compressed yeast
3 tbsps. honey

1 tbsp. sea salt
4¼ cups unbleached unsifted
  flour
1 gallon boiling water

Warm large mixing bowl. Add warm water to bowl; sprinkle or crumble yeast over water to dissolve, stirring. Stir in honey, salt, and enough flour to form a soft dough. Turn out on lightly floured board; knead 10 minutes until dough is smooth and elastic. Cover, let rise in warm place, free from drafts, 15 minutes. Punch down dough. Roll out dough on lightly floured board into a 5- × 9-inch rectangle. Dough should be 1 inch thick. Cut into 12 equal strips. Roll each strip until ½ inch thick. Moisten ends, join together to form bagels. Cover, let rise in warm place 20 minutes. Drop 4 or 5 bagels into boiling water. Simmer bagels exactly 7 minutes (longer will cause sogginess). Remove; cool on towel. Cook remaining bagels. Bake bagels on ungreased cookie sheet in preheated 375° F. oven 30 to 35 minutes. Cool to eat. Or wrap and freeze until ready to use. Makes 1 dozen bagels.

BAGEL LUNCH/BRUNCH requires plenty of bagels and fixings from your favorite "deli," or your refrigerator—and lots of imagination! Keep it informal. Do it in the kitchen where broiler or toaster is handy to buffet table.

JEWISH ENGLISH BAGEL: Toast bagel; top with sour cream or cream cheese, jam, or preserves. Terrific for breakfast or snacking!

HERO BAGELS: Bring on cold cuts (cold sliced roast beef, baked or boiled ham, turkey), Swiss or American sliced cheese, slivered lettuce or cabbage, mild or "hot" mustard to build a hero bagel. Great for all heroes and heroines!

PEANUT-APPLE BAGEL: Spread hot, toasted, buttered bagel with peanut butter; top with thin slices of crisp red apple. Boon to vegetarians!

SHRIMPY BAGELS: Garnish slices of hard-cooked egg and shrimps with dollops of mayonnaise and capers on bed of shredded lettuce on split bagels.

"TERRIBLY ENGLISH": Cut cucumber into thin slices. Place on top of bagel (split in half) spread lightly with mayonnaise. Top with crisp watercress.

BAGELS AND LOX: Traditional old favorite! Bagel sandwich made with cream cheese and paper-thin slices of smoked salmon. Can't be beat!

BAGEL BURGER: Split bagel in half. Top with lean ground beef and slice of American or aged Cheddar cheese. Run under broiler. Lather lavishly with catsup or prepared yellow mustard. Garnish with onion rings. Best yet!

DEVILED BAGEL: Split bagel; spread with deviled luncheon meat. Top with sour cream or plain yogurt. Garnish with snipped dill or parsley. Tasty for devils, small or large, old or young!

TOMATO-CHEESE BAGEL: Split bagel; spread with horseradish or mustard. Top with thin slices of Swiss or Cheddar cheese. Run under broiler until cheese is bubbly. Top with thinly sliced beefsteak tomato. Only delicious!

CALIFORNIA CAESAR SALAD

1 cup peanut oil
1 clove garlic, pressed
2 cups Italian bread cubes
2 heads romaine lettuce
1 head iceberg lettuce
1 bunch watercress
¾ cup freshly grated
  Parmesan or Romano
  cheese
½ tsp. sea salt

¼ tsp. dry mustard
¼ tsp. freshly ground black
  pepper
⅓ cup fresh lemon juice
2 eggs, lightly beaten
dash Worcestershire sauce
1 can (2 oz.) anchovy fillets

Pour oil into jar. Add garlic. Cover; let stand 1 hour. Use ¼ cup of garlic oil to sauté bread cubes until golden. Tear romaine, lettuce, and watercress into a large salad bowl. Sprinkle with Parmesan (or Romano) cheese, salt, mustard, and pepper. Pour on remaining oil, lemon juice, and eggs. Add Worcestershire sauce, fillets, and bread cubes. Toss lightly until well mixed. Serves 10 to 12.

CARROTS 'N GRAPES

6 cups coarsely shredded
  carrots *
⅓ cup margarine
¼ tsp. anise seed
1 tsp. sea salt

1 tsp. honey
4 tbsps. water
3 cups seedless green
  grapes

Combine carrots, margarine, anise, salt, honey, and water in a 2-quart saucepan. Cover, cook 5 minutes or until carrots are tender. Stir in grapes. Serve piping hot! Serves 6.

NOTE: Colorful, low-caloried, and tasteful, this vegetable/fruit side dish is loaded with vitamins, too!

SECOND DECAN: MAY 31 to JUNE 10

Add the qualities of Venus to Mercury, and bring on those beautiful Venusian tree-ripe fruits for picnics, Sunday outings, or midnight snacking. Since you seem more cheerful, generous, and artistic, you enjoy quick outdoor cookouts with friends and family.

You have many acquaintances but few close friends. Don't overlook things that could turn off your friends. Keep them happy with a barbecue under sunny skies in the patio or back yard.

BURGERS DELISH! *

Guacamole *

Florentine Salad *   Home Fries *

Watermelon Boat *: pears,* cherries,* blueberries,* bananas, grapes, * and strawberries *

Perfect Iced Tea *

BURGERS DELISH!

1½ lbs. ground chuck
1½ tsps. salt
¼ tsp. freshly ground black
   pepper
3 tbsps. milk

¾ cup crushed corn chips
1 loaf French bread, sliced
   and buttered
Guacamole, optional

Toss meat lightly with salt, pepper, milk, and corn chips. Shape into 8 patties. Grill over hot coals 4 to 5 minutes. Serve on French bread. Top with Guacamole if desired. Serves 8.

GUACAMOLE

1 ripe large California
   avocado, peeled, pitted
½ tsp. salad oil
½ tsp. seasoned salt
dash of cayenne

1 tbsp. instant minced
   onion
1 tbsp. mayonnaise
1 tbsp. fresh lemon juice
1 small tomato, chopped

Mash avocado with fork; blend in seasonings. Beat until creamy. Fold in tomato. Makes about 2 cups.

FLORENTINE SALAD

1 clove garlic, crushed
¾ cup salad oil
½ cup red wine vinegar
½ tsp. sea salt
dash freshly ground black
    pepper
⅛ tsp. honey
1 pint cherry tomatoes,
    halved

1 lb. fresh spinach
¼ lb. (1 or 2 heads) Belgian
    endive, optional
2 hard-cooked eggs,
    chopped
3 slices fried bacon,
    crumbled

Combine garlic, salad oil, vinegar, salt, pepper, and honey. Add halved cherry tomatoes; marinate 1 hour or more. Wash spinach well, drain; tear into pieces; arrange with endive in salad bowl. Refrigerate salad greens. When ready to serve, add tomatoes with dressing to salad greens; toss lightly. Sprinkle chopped eggs and bacon over all. Serves 8.

HOME FRIES

⅓ cup salad oil
5 cups pared, sliced
    potatoes

1 cup sliced onions
sea salt and pepper

Heat oil in large heavy skillet. Arrange potatoes and onions in single layers in skillet. Sprinkle each layer with salt, pepper. Cover, cook over low heat 20 minutes. Uncover, cook over medium heat about 10 minutes or until crispy brown on underside. (Do not stir.) Turn over, brown on other side. Serves 8.

PERFECT ICED TEA *

Fill 1 quart pitcher with cold tap water. Add 8 to 10 tea bags. Cover with lid; let stand at room temperature or in refrigerator at least 6 hours or overnight. Remove tea bags, pour into ice-filled glasses. Serves 6.

NOTE: This is the most perfect way to make cloudless tea (ruled by Mercury). For 10 to 12 servings, double recipe using 2 qts. water.

THIRD DECAN: JUNE 11 to JUNE 20

Due to its influence, your moods also seem to wax and wane like the moon. You are quick and adaptable in the kitchen, whipping up carrot cake for special treats to celebrate the end of the school year and the beginning of summer. But don't let your tendency to be forgetful allow the family larder to become depleted.

Lunar astrological foods include watercress,* cucumbers,* pumpkins,* lettuce* and cashew nuts.* Put it all together and it's a great time for a way-out wingding!

AVOCADO AND SPROUTS SANDWICH *

- or -

INCREDIBLY GOOD EGG SCRAMBLE *

Watercress *-Lettuce *-Cucumber * Salad with

Poppy Seed Salad Dressing *

Bing Cherries *   Honeydew Melon *

Carrot Cake * with Honey Cream Cheese Icing *

- or -

LAMB STEW RUMANIAN *

Hot Savory Green Bean Salad *

Olive's Swedish Rye Bread *   Sweet Butter

Apples   Bananas   Cashews *

AVOCADO AND SPROUTS SANDWICH

2 *slices whole-wheat bread*
1 *tbsp. mayonnaise*
½ *cup alfalfa sprouts*
2 *slices tomato*
2 *slices Swiss, Cheddar, or*
  Jack cheese

Caraway, sesame, or
  sunflower seeds
2 *thick slices California*
  avocado

Spread mayonnaise over 1 side of each bread slice. Layer about ¼ cup alfalfa sprouts over each slice. Add tomatoes and cheese for open-face sandwich. Sprinkle with seeds. Broil until cheese melts. Top with avocado slices. Makes 1 sandwich.

INCREDIBLY GOOD EGG SCRAMBLE

For each person allow:

2 eggs
1½ tbsps. cream or milk
sea salt, freshly ground

black pepper
or white pepper to taste
1 tbsp. sweet butter

Beat eggs lightly with cream and seasonings. Pour into melted butter in skillet. Cook, stirring constantly over low heat until eggs begin to firm up but are still "wet." Turn out on heated plates. Serve with fried toast triangles, toasted English muffins, croutons, or fried tortillas.

And now the scramble is on—select flavorful ingredients to give zest to your eggs. Let your imagination be your guide. Ad-lib the rest. The results are incredible!

FISH FLAVORS: Add caviar, lemon, and Tabasco to beaten eggs just before mixture thickens. Top with sour cream, chopped chives. Or use slivered smoked salmon, tiny cooked baby shrimps, tuna, salmon, crab, or lobster meat. Garnish with cut lemon. Serve with hot buttered toast or sardines and lemon slices.

VEGETABLE VARIATIONS: Add sautéed artichoke hearts, mushrooms (fresh or canned), butter-fried eggplant. Or spinach (or chicory or sorrel) lightly cooked in salted water; drain, flavor with nutmeg, lemon butter. Or fried chopped sweet peppers and/or pimientos in vegetable oil. Or add peeled diced tomatoes to scrambled eggs.

MISCELLANY: Cut fresh herbs (parsley, chives, chervil, basil, tarragon); add to eggs during cooking. Snip few extra herbs over the top of scrambled eggs for added flavor. Incorporate cheese, either mild (cream) or aromatic (Limburger), or garnish with grated Parmesan or Romano. Give added zing with toasted caraway, sesame, or sunflower seeds; seasoned salts from lemon pepper to celery salt to off-beat condiments: tarragon-flavored vinegar, Worcestershire sauce, "hot" catsup or steak sauce. Anything goes!

POPPY SEED SALAD DRESSING

2 tbsps. dry mustard
2 tbsps. water
¾ cup honey
1 tbsp. poppy seed

2 tsps. instant minced
onion
1 tsp. sea salt
1 cup salad or olive oil
⅓ cup vinegar

Blend together mustard with water; let stand 10 minutes for flavor to develop. Combine with honey, poppy seed, onion, salt, and oil. Beat with rotary beater until thickened. Makes 1½ cups.

CARROT CAKE

1½ cups vegetable oil
2 cups raw sugar or
1½ cups honey
4 eggs
2 cups unbleached flour
2 tsps. baking soda
2 tsps. baking powder

2 tsps. cinnamon
1 tsp. sea salt
3 cups finely shredded
carrots
1 cup chopped hazelnuts,
pecans, or California
walnuts

Combine vegetable oil and sugar (or honey), beating until well blended. Add 1 egg at a time, mix well after each addition. Sift together dry ingredients. Add to cake batter, beating until smooth. Stir in carrots and nuts. Beat batter ½ minute. Pour mixture into 3 well-greased, lightly floured, round 9-inch layer tins. Bake in preheated 300° F. oven 45 minutes (or until cake tester inserted in center comes out clean). Cool in pans 10 minutes. Turn out on wire racks to cool. Frost with honey cream cheese icing. Serves 10 to 12.

HONEY CREAM CHEESE ICING

1 pkg. (8 oz.) cream cheese   *4 tsps. pure vanilla extract*
1 stick butter   *⅓ cup honey*
               confectioners' sugar

Whip together cream cheese and butter until fluffy. Add vanilla; beat in honey until well blended. Gradually add enough confectioners' sugar to make smooth icing, stiff enough to spread on cake. Put layers together with frosting; frost outside of cake.

NOTE: Rich and wonderful! Fantastic for anyone who is lucky enough to rate a carrot cake to honor his or her birthday.

LAMB STEW RUMANIAN

8 *parsnips, peeled, cut*
  in chunks
2 *large turnips,* * *peeled,*
  cut in chunks
6 *large carrots,* * *peeled,*
  cut in large pieces
3 *small yellow onions,*
  diced
4 *lean shoulder lamb*
  chops, bone out, cut in
  large pieces
water or canned chicken
  stock

1 *tsp. paprika*
½ *tsp. dill weed* *
½ *tsp. summer savory* *
small bunch of kale,
  washed, chopped
4 *small new potatoes,*
  well scrubbed (jackets
  left on)
sea salt, pepper to taste
⅓ *cup unbleached flour*
dairy sour cream or plain
  yogurt, optional

Put all ingredients in stewing pot except flour and sour cream. Bring to boil; simmer, covered, 45 minutes or until lamb and vegetables are tender. Remove 1 cup liquid from stewing pot; mix with flour to form smooth paste. Return flour-water mixture to pot. Stir and cook until thickened and flour is cooked. Taste to correct seasonings. Serve alone or with sour cream or yogurt. Perfect with Swedish rye bread! Serves 4.

AFTERTHOUGHTS: A substantial meal-in-one when the Gemini cook is in the mood! The hearty stew, rich in protein, vitamins, and minerals, stars four astrological foods: savory, dill, turnips, and carrots!

HOT SAVORY GREEN BEAN SALAD

1 lb. fresh green beans
boiling salted water
4 slices lean bacon, diced
½ cup minced green onions
2 tbsps. tarragon vinegar

2 tbsps. minced fresh
*savory ***
salt, white pepper to taste
1 tbsp. minced fresh
parsley

Blanch beans in large kettle of boiling salted water about 8 minutes. Drain; cool under running cold water. Trim ends, cut in fine diagonal slices. Fry bacon until crisp; remove bacon bits with slotted spoon. Saute onions in bacon drippings until tender; stir in tarragon vinegar and 1 tbsp. savory. Toss beans with herb mixture; season to taste with salt and white pepper. Heat until beans are tender and hot. Sprinkle on bacon bits and 1 tbsp. tarragon and parsley. Serve at once. Serves 3 to 4.

AFTERTHOUGHTS: The well-known herbalist, Culpeper, advised his readers, "Keep savory by you all the year if you love yourself and your ease!" German gardeners and cooks so love the herb, they call it *Bohnenkraut* or "bean herb." It's great for meats and fish, too.

OLIVE'S SWEDISH RYE BREAD

2 pkgs. active dry yeast
2 cups water
4⅓ tbsps. white sugar
7½ to 8 cups unbleached
    flour
2 cups milk
5 tbsps. butter
½ cup brown sugar

1 tbsp. sea salt
½ cup dark molasses or
    honey
1 tsp. anise seed
1 tsp. fennel seed *
1 tsp. caraway seed *
grated rind of 1 orange
3 cups rye flour

Form yeast sponge by dissolving yeast in 1 cup lukewarm water
with 1 tsp. sugar and 1 cup unbleached flour. Form smooth
paste; let mixture rise 30 minutes in warm place. Meanwhile,
combine in large saucepan milk, 1 cup water, butter, brown
sugar, remaining 4 tbsps. sugar, salt, molasses (or honey), anise
seed, fennel seed, caraway seed, and orange rind. Mix well;
bring to boil. Cool. Add all rye flour, 1 cup unbleached flour to
cooled milk-spice mixture. Mix well; add yeast sponge, beating
hard. Add 2 more cups unbleached flour; work into soft dough.
It will take additional 3½ to 4 cups unbleached flour to form an
elastic, stiff dough. Turn out on lightly floured board as soon as
it is possible to knead and incorporate unbleached flour. Knead
vigorously. Put into greased bowl; turn to grease top. Cover, let
rise in warm place, free from drafts, until doubled in bulk.
Shape into 3 equal-sized loaves. Place dough in greased 5- ×
10-inch bread pans. Let dough rise in pans to double in bulk.
Bake in preheated 375° F. oven 45 minutes (or until bread
sounds hollow when thumped with fingers). Cool on wire racks
a few minutes before removing from pans. Grease crusts with
soft butter. Makes 3 loaves.

NOTE: Stupendous! Freezes well if there is anything left! Recipe
comes from Swedish household. Bread is traditionally dipped
in simmering meat juices (gathered from the pre-Christmas
holiday cooking) by stabbing hunks of bread with a fork before

soaking it in stock pot! Bread is sweet when toasted. Makes deliciously different sandwiches made with smoked tongue, smoked Swedish cheese, lingonberries (tart red berries similar to cranberries) and topped with grated beet root. Try it!

CANCER: JUNE 21 to JULY 22

You Take the Cake!

SINCE YOU'RE A CHILD of the moon and the crab creature of the sea, you are devoted to domestic things. Any kitchen task is a labor of love. French chocolate soufflé or black bottom pie is your kind of dish. Even moon men excel in the kitchen, often making catering their vocation.

You don't know any half measure in love or in the culinary arts. Like many Cancerians, you are often very possessive (you'll take the very last piece of cake left on the plate). Your extreme sensitivity and excellent memory make you a fine host or hostess, willing to devote long hours in the kitchen putting your natural talent to work to create the special dish to please the most discerning palate.

Just one word of caution though: you are never at your best when there's tension in the kitchen, for it can lead to incessant worry and digestive upsets. Too often you worry about having enough food to feed your friends. You prepare too much and then gorge yourself on the leftovers.

You shine on Monday and Friday, so entertain your friends and loved ones on those days.

FIRST DECAN: JUNE 21 to JULY 1

Cancer subjects are ruled by the moon and its resulting tides, so it's small wonder they have a passion for anything that swims!

You often worry about having enough food to feed your best friends. Since you prepare too much and can't bear having left-overs, invariably you nibble at the leftovers—adding to your waistline. So, if you move into the field of Cancer menus, beware! To beat the problem, drink plenty of water and milk; keep meats to the minimum; substitute calcium-rich cheese and vegetables. Eat fruits and vegetables, especially those high in water content like your astrological foods: watercress,* lettuce,* cucumbers,* melons,* pumpkins,* turnips,* and cabbage.*

Now is the time to bring on yummy desserts, especially for friends. Scorpios who dig gourmet fare and Leonians who adore food presented with pomp and circumstance will be impressed with your cooking!

———

PEAR SALMON PAPRIKASH *

Cucumbers,* Country Style *   Corn on the Cob

Celestial Chocolate Mousse *

- or -

CANCERIAN DANDY IN ASPIC *

Venusian Zucchini * Thyme Bake *   Pumpkin * Bread *

Summer Fruit Cooler *

Buttermilk

PEAR SALMON PAPRIKASH

2 fresh California Bartlett
  pears
4 salmon steaks, weighing
  about 2 lbs.
1 cup dry white wine
unbleached flour

sea salt, freshly ground
  black pepper
dash paprika
¼ cup butter or margarine
minced fresh parsley
lemon wedges

Cut pears lengthwise into halves; remove cores with melon
baller or small spoon. Marinate salmon in wine 15 minutes;
turn, marinate 15 minutes longer. Dry, shake with flour, salt,
and pepper to coat steaks. Sprinkle with paprika. Brown both
sides in butter or margarine, add wine marinade. Arrange pears
around salmon. Simmer, covered, 10 minutes until fish flakes
and pears are tender but not soft. Serve with minced parsley
and lemon wedges for garnish. Serves 4.

CUCUMBERS,* COUNTRY STYLE

1 tbsp. unbleached flour
1 tbsp. fine dry bread
  crumbs
¼ tsp. sea salt
  few gratings freshly
  ground black pepper

pinch garlic powder
1½ cups thinly sliced
  unpeeled cucumbers *
2 tbsps. salad oil

Combine flour, bread crumbs, and seasonings. Dredge cucumbers with flour mixture. Heat oil in skillet. Add cucumbers; brown on both sides. Drain on absorbent paper. Serve at once. Serves 4.

CELESTIAL CHOCOLATE MOUSSE

2 envelopes (2 tbsps.)
  unflavored gelatin
1 cup sugar, divided
¼ tsp. sea salt
4 eggs, separated
2 cups milk

2 pkgs. (6 oz. each)
  semisweet real chocolate
  pieces
2 tsps. pure vanilla extract
2 cups heavy cream,
  whipped

Combine gelatin, ½ cup sugar, and salt in 3-quart saucepan. Beat together egg yolks and milk; stir into gelatin mixture. Add chocolate pieces. Cook over medium heat, stirring constantly, until gelatin is dissolved and chocolate is melted. Remove from heat; stir in vanilla extract. Chill, stirring occasionally, until mixture mounds when dropped from a spoon. Beat egg whites until stiff, but not dry. Gradually add remaining sugar; beat until very stiff. Fold in chocolate mixture. Fold in whipped cream. Turn into 2-quart decorative mold. Chill until firm. Unmold. If desired, garnish with whipped cream. Serves 16.

NOTE: My celestial dessert is the perfect dessert to serve your favorite Leonian! Ancient Aztecs, according to legend, who worshiped the sun god, believed that Lualzoucoult, the gardener of Eden where the first sun children lived, was the one who bought the seeds of the "Guacalmolt"—the cocoa * tree—to earth!

CANCERIAN DANDY IN ASPIC

2 or 3 fresh California
  Bartlett pears
1 can (1 lb.) salmon
2 pkgs. (3 oz. each) lemon-
  flavored gelatin
1 cup boiling water
¼ cup vinegar

2 tbsps. minced chives
½ tsp. sea salt
⅛ tsp. white pepper
ice or ice water
3 or 4 eggs, deviled
watercress

Core, shred pears to measure 2 cups. Drain salmon, reserve liquid. Remove salmon skin and bones; coarsely crumble fish. Dissolve gelatin in boiling water; add reserved salmon liquid, vinegar, chives, salt, and pepper. Add ice or ice water to measure 1 quart. Combine with pear and salmon. Pour into 1½-quart fish or plain mold. Chill until firm. Unmold onto platter. Arrange eggs around mold; garnish with watercress. Serves 6 to 8.

VENUSIAN ZUCCHINI * THYME BAKE

3 tbsps. olive oil
1 clove garlic
4 medium zucchini * cut in
thin slices
¼ tsp. thyme
¼ tsp. oregano
½ cup freshly grated
Parmesan or Romano
cheese

4 tomatoes peeled and
sliced
sea salt
freshly ground black
pepper
4 tbsps. bread crumbs
mixed with 2 tbsps.
melted butter

Heat olive oil in skillet; sauté garlic in oil few minutes. Lift out garlic bud, discard. Add zucchini to skillet, sauté over low heat few minutes. Combine thyme, oregano, and cheese. In well-greased casserole alternate layers of zucchini, cheese, and tomato slices. Sprinkle with salt and pepper to taste. Repeat layers. Top with buttered bread crumbs. Bake uncovered in preheated 350° F. oven for 30 minutes or until browned on top. Serves 4.

AFTERTHOUGHTS: Governed by Venus, thyme is often called "the manger herb" because the Christ Child is said to have slept on a bed of fragrant hay that contained the fragrant thyme. There are many varieties, but *Thymus vulgaris* is our concern. Thyme is a symbol of activity. It grows profusely in New England meadows, a runaway from colonial times. Burned as incense in ancient temples to purify and scent the air. Roman soldiers often bathed in it to acquire courage and strength and the spontaneous emotion needed in battle. Today it is often used to scent linens or make a potpourri. Popularly used as charms and in incantations. The "cure-all" herb is supposed to end hangovers, nightmares, melancholy, and digestive troubles. It is one of the basic ingredients in the French cooking herb blend *bouquet garni* for flavoring soups, fish, and stews.

PUMPKIN * BREAD

1 large can (16 oz.) pumpkin * or 2 cups fresh cooked pumpkin *	2¾ cups unbleached flour
	6 tsps. baking powder
	4 tsps. cloves
2⅓ cups honey	1¼ tsps. cinnamon
1 cup vegetable oil	dash sea salt
2 eggs	1 cup water
2¼ cups whole wheat flour	2 cups chopped walnuts
	2 cups raisins

Mix together pumpkin, honey, oil, and eggs. Add dry ingredients (sifted together) alternately with water. Add nuts and raisins if desired. Bake 1 hour in preheated 350° F. oven in 3 well-greased loaf pans. Makes 3 loaves.

SUMMER FRUIT COOLER

2 fresh pears	2 tbsps. fresh lemon or lime juice
2 cups watermelon balls *	8 sugar-frosted mint sprigs

Core pears, cut into chunks. Toss with melon balls and lemon or lime juice. Chill. Moisten mint lightly with water or slightly beaten egg white and coat with powdered or granulated sugar. Garnish each serving with a mint sprig. Serves 8.

AFTERTHOUGHTS: Expand this delightful summer cooler into a main course fruit plate! Add scoops of cottage cheese, wedges of cantaloupe and honeydew melon, clumps of seedless green grapes, fresh whole strawberries, nectarines, or ripe plums. The results are delightfully delicious!

SECOND DECAN: JULY 2 to JULY 11

Add to the moon the qualities of Mars and you'll discover you're forceful, daring, courageous, impatient, and often destructive. It's therefore best for you to rely on foods from the sea or simple chops or steaks to grill or bake that require little preparation but provide delightful eating.

Due to your Martian-type nature, you'll thrive on "hot" salads or vegetables enlivened by the addition of cayenne,* pepper,* onion,* chives,* radishes,* and mustard.* When you dine out, you often choose chili parlors serving the spiciest chili in town! Hot tamales or tacos from a Mexican food roadside are a great appetite appeaser for moon children with the daring of Mars! Remember to cool it all down with the proper balance of bland, calcium-rich foods such as buttermilk and cottage cheese.

Select your dinner guests very carefully during this period. Typically, you are happiest with your fellow water signs, Scorpios and Pisceans, but sometimes ill at ease with Arieans and Librans.

HERBED STEAKS *

Parslied * Potatoes   Cabbage Chinese Style *

Scrumptious Fourth House Salad * with Olive French Dressing *

Fresh Raspberry Tarts *   Lemon-Minted Tea

- or -

STUFFED SOUTH AFRICAN ROCK LOBSTER TAILS *
or Chicken Salad, Chinese *

Stir-Fried Chinese Lettuce *　　　Garden Peas

Fresh Rhubarb * Pie

HERBED STEAKS

For basting sauce:

4 tbsps. olive oil	1 tsp. minced fresh
4 tbsps. red wine vinegar	rosemary
2 tsps. minced fresh thyme	sea salt, freshly ground
	black pepper to taste

Combine all ingredients; set aside.

For steaks:

2 porterhouse or sirloin steaks, salt, freshly ground black pepper. Rub steaks on both sides with salt and pepper. Broil steaks, brushing lightly several times with basting sauce. Turn, broil on other side to desired doneness. Serve at once. Serves 6 to 8.

NOTE: Dried herbs may be substituted for fresh herbs.

CABBAGE CHINESE STYLE

1 small head cabbage *	sea salt, freshly ground
2 scant tbsps. butter or	black pepper to taste
salad oil	about 1 tbsp. water,
	optional

Cut cabbage into fine shreds with Chinese vegetable cleaver or sharp knife. Heat butter or salad oil in Chinese wok or large skillet. Add shredded cabbage, salt, and pepper to taste. Stir-fry cabbage for a few minutes until cabbage begins to become limp. For desired "softer" bite, add water, cook about 1 minute longer. Serve at once. Serves 6 to 8.

NOTE: Cabbage should never be overcooked but should come out a gorgeous grass-green color. White pepper makes a lovely seasoning especially to suit the palate of discerning Scorpios!

SCRUMPTIOUS FOURTH HOUSE SALAD

1 *head western iceberg
  lettuce, cleaned and crisp*
4 *radishes,* sliced*
1 *cucumber, cut in thin
  slices*
4 *large mushrooms,
  washed, pat-dried, thinly
  sliced*
small red onion, peeled,
  cut in rings*
2 *garden-ripe tomatoes,
  cut in wedges*

1 *small ripe avocado, cut in
  rings*
*few drops fresh lemon juice
good bottled diet dressing
  or olive French
  Dressing **
*sea salt and freshly ground
  black pepper*

Combine lettuce, radishes, cucumbers, mushrooms, and tomatoes in large salad bowl. Toss gently. Add avocado rings, moisten lightly with lemon juice. Pour small amount of diet or olive French dressing. Toss lightly. Season liberally with salt and pepper just before serving. Serves 4.

OLIVE FRENCH DRESSING

⅔ *cup corn oil*
¼ *cup dry sherry*
3 *tbsps. fresh lemon juice*
1 *tbsp. bottled salad
  dressing*

2 *tbsps. frozen or freeze-
  dried chopped chives **
dash of honey
½ *cup chopped ripe olives*

Combine all ingredients in jar, cover tightly. Shake vigorously to blend. Shake again just before pouring over salad greens. Makes about 1⅓ cups.

FRESH RASPBERRY TARTS

6 baked 3-inch tart shells
⅓ cup honey
2 tbsps. cornstarch
dash sea salt
1⅛ cups milk
1 pkg. (3 oz.) cream
  cheese, softened

1 egg yolk, lightly beaten
½ tsp. pure vanilla extract
1 egg white
2 tbsps. vanilla sugar
sugared fresh raspberries
fresh mint leaves

Bake tart shells from one-crust pastry recipe; cool thoroughly. In saucepan, combine honey, cornstarch, and salt. Add 1 cup milk. Cook and stir over medium heat until thickened. Remove from heat. Combine cream cheese, remaining milk, and egg yolk. Slowly add cream cheese mixture to hot pudding, stirring constantly. Return to heat; cook and stir 2 minutes longer. Stir in vanilla; set aside. Beat egg white to form soft peaks. Gradually add vanilla sugar, beating to form stiff peaks. Fold into pudding. Spoon into tart shells; chill. To serve: arrange sugared berries atop pudding. Garnish each with fresh mint leaves if desired. Serves 6.

NOTE: Vanilla sugar is a lovely way to perfume and flavor fruit. To prepare vanilla sugar, cut 1-inch piece of vanilla pod and bury it in a canister of granulated sugar. Cover canister. Wait several days before using. If desired, tarts can be made with a combination of fruits such as peaches, nectarines, or blueberries.

STUFFED SOUTH AFRICAN ROCK LOBSTER TAILS

*3 pkgs. (8 oz. each) frozen
South African rock
lobster tails*
*1 cup finely diced bread
cubes*
*1 tsp. minced onion ***
*2 tbsps. minced parsley ***

½ cup mayonnaise
1 tsp. Worcestershire sauce
*2 egg yolks, hard-cooked,
sieved*
2 egg whites, stiffly beaten
*½ cup grated Parmesan
cheese*

Parboil frozen rock lobster tails by dropping into boiling salted water. When water reboils, drain immediately and drench with cold water. Remove lower skin; discard. Remove meat from shell and dice. Reserve shells. Toss rock lobster meat with bread cubes, onion,* parsley,* mayonnaise, Worcestershire sauce, and egg yolks. Use mixture to stuff shells. Place filled shells on cookie sheet. Fold together egg whites and Parmesan cheese. Spoon mixture over rock lobster stuffing. Bake in preheated 350° F. oven 20 minutes or until topping is golden brown. Sprinkle with additional grated Parmesan cheese. Garnish with lemon slices. Serves 6.

CHICKEN SALAD, CHINESE

1 *medium-sized head
western iceberg lettuce* *
4 *scallions*
6 *tbsps. soy sauce*
2 *tbsps. honey*
2 *tbsps. salad oil*
4 *cups cooked chicken,
slivered*
¼ *cup parsley, chopped*

¼ *lb. Chinese Fun
See (cellophane noodles
or vermicelli)
oil for frying*
1 *cup roasted blanched
almonds or*
1 *tbsp. toasted sesame
seeds, chopped
or slivered*

Core, rinse, and thoroughly drain lettuce; refrigerate in disposable plastic bag. Cut scallions into thin slivers 2 inches long. Combine soy sauce, honey, and salad oil; stir. Mix with chicken. Shortly before serving, shred lettuce into large bowl, add scallions and parsley.* Cook noodles (or vermicelli) in boiling salted water 3 minutes; drain well. Heat ½ inch oil in skillet; add noodles (or vermicelli) in one piece and cook until browned on one side (about 4 minutes); turn and cook second side until browned (about ½ minute). Drain well on absorbent paper. Add chicken and dressing to lettuce. Break up noodles (or vermicelli) over top and add almonds or sesame seeds. Toss until well mixed. Serve at once. Serves 8.

NOTE: Cellophane noodles, also known as bean threads or Chinese noodles, are found in Oriental food shops. A beautiful, light dish, slightly esoteric, but a terrific way to use up leftover chicken or turkey.

STIR-FRIED CHINESE LETTUCE

2 *heads western iceberg
lettuce*
1 *scant tbsp. olive or salad
oil*

*sea salt
freshly ground black
pepper
few drops wine vinegar*

Wash, core lettuce. Drain well. Heat oil in wok or large skillet.
Add lettuce (torn into pieces). Stir-fry quickly, barely ½ minute.
Season to taste with salt, pepper. Serve hot in salad bowl; toss
lightly with wine vinegar. Terrific way to have your salad greens
hot!

THIRD DECAN: JULY 12 to JULY 22

Add to the moon the qualities of the sun—dignity, pride, dependability, faithfulness, conceit, and a desire for power. Now is an ideal time for showing off your cooking prowess. Do it outdoors, performing over the rotisserie or at the seaside near the shore. For the outdoor bash—the male Cancerian excels here—choose shish kabob, marinated in a special sauce, or barbecued chicken. Or from the sea, create a luscious oyster stuffing for a baked bass.

Since all Cancerians love the outdoors, choose salad greens from your own favorite meadow, yellow with the blaze of dandelions.* For a healthful nibble, sunflower seeds * make delicious, nutritional eating—either alone or to sprinkle on salads.

Above all, enjoy the midsummer harvest of a gorgeous array of garden-ripe fruits and vegetables. Since you're lazy from basking in the rays of Mr. Sol, cook early, serve later in the day.

BARBECUED CHICKEN *

Green Beans, Crisp and Tender   Kraut Bread
with Herb Butter *

Dandelion Salad with Hot Dressing *

Chilled Wedges of Watermelon

Backyard Hand-Churned Homemade Strawberry Ice Cream *

BARBECUED CHICKEN

¾ *cup catsup*
1 *tbsp. prepared mustard*
⅔ *cup drained sweet pickle*
  relish
2 *tbsps. soy sauce*
2 *tbsps. honey*

1 *clove garlic, crushed*
⅛ *tsp. freshly ground black*
  pepper
2 *broiler-fryer chickens,*
  each about 3 lbs., cut in
  serving pieces

Blend together catsup and mustard in small bowl. Add remaining ingredients except chicken. Mix thoroughly. Set sauce aside. Grill chicken about 8 inches from low coals for 35 minutes. Turn with tongs occasionally. When chicken has grilled 35 minutes, brush both sides with sauce and continue grilling for additional 25 minutes or until chicken is tender. Brush and turn occasionally. Serves 6 to 8.

NOTE: To test temperature of a charcoal briquet fire, cautiously hold your hand, palm side down, just above the grill. Judge temperature by number of seconds hand can be kept in position. For this recipe, your hand should be kept in position for 4 seconds. To lower temperature, tap the outer gray layer from coals and push coals closer together. If more coals are needed, add them to outer edge of hot coals.

HERB BUTTER

Combine 1 cup butter (room temperature), ¼ tsp. caraway seed, ⅛ tsp. thyme leaves, and ⅛ tsp. marjoram. Let stand at room temperature 1 hour before using.

KRAUT BREAD WITH HERB BUTTER

¾ cup drained
    sauerkraut
3 tbsps. butter
    or margarine
¼ cup sliced scallions
½ cup shredded carrots
½ tsp. caraway seed
1½ tsps. honey

dash freshly ground
    black pepper
¼ tsp. sea salt
2 tbsps. chopped parsley *
2 cups prepared biscuit mix
⅔ cup milk

Place kraut on several layers of paper toweling. Press to remove as much moisture as possible. Melt butter or margarine in large skillet, sauté scallions, carrots, and kraut in skillet 5 minutes, stirring occasionally. Remove from heat; stir in caraway seed, honey, pepper, salt, and parsley.* In bowl, combine biscuit mix and milk. Turn dough onto floured board and knead lightly 4 or 5 times. Roll out to a rectangle 12 × 16 inches. Sprinkle kraut mixture evenly over surface of dough. Roll up, jelly-roll fashion, starting with long side. Place roll, seam side down, on ungreased baking sheet. Shape roll into a horseshoe. Tuck ends of roll under so filling is not exposed. If desired, brush bread with a beaten egg and sprinkle with caraway seed. Bake in preheated 375° F. oven 30 minutes. Serve warm with herb butter. Serves 6 to 8.

DANDELION * SALAD WITH HOT DRESSING

For the salad:

*2 quarts cleaned dandelion greens * cut in ½-inch pieces*

½ small white onion, peeled, minced
sea salt, freshly ground black pepper

For the "hot dressing":

4 pieces of lean bacon, finely diced

4 tbsps. wine vinegar
sea salt, freshly ground pepper to taste

Place greens, onion, salt, and pepper in large salad bowl. Add dressing and toss lightly to serve. Serves 6.

NOTE: Exact recipe for dandelion greens will depend on palate of the cook! For sharper flavor, increase amount of bacon, bacon fat, vinegar, salt, and pepper. It's a terrific way to pick up your greens while adding vitamins A and C and iron to your diet. Go pick them and eat them, out in the shining sun!

BACKYARD HAND-CHURNED HOMEMADE STRAWBERRY ICE CREAM

2 *pints fresh strawberries*	*1 tbsp. vanilla extract*
2 *cups honey*	*3 cups heavy cream*
6 *egg yolks*	*red food coloring,*
½ *tsp. sea salt*	*optional*
3 *cups scalded milk*	

Wash, hull strawberries. Purée strawberries by whirling in electric blender until liquified or by pressing through sieve. Mix with 1 cup honey. Let stand in refrigerator at least 1 hour. To prepare custard, beat together egg yolks, remaining honey, and salt. Slowly stir in scalded milk. Pour into medium-sized saucepan and stir over medium heat until mixture coats a metal spoon. Remove from heat; add vanilla and cool; stir in cream and food coloring. Chill. Combine chilled custard with puréed strawberries. Freeze ice cream in 4-quart electric freezer or hand-churn ice-cream freezer according to manufacturer's instructions or use directions given below. Makes 4 quarts.

TO CHURN ICE CREAM:

Fit dasher into freezer canister; pour strawberry ice cream mixture into canister (canister should be no more than ⅔ full to allow for expansion). Cover canister with lid, place in freezer tub. Set freezer tub in pan or sink to catch ice water as it drains off through holes. Clamp gear frame to dasher; pack freezer tub with alternate layers of crushed ice and rock salt, using 1 quart crushed ice per ⅓ cup rock salt. Do not let ice or rock salt reach top of canister. If using hand churn, turn crank slowly 5 minutes; increase speed and continue to crank until handle is difficult to turn. If using electric churn, allow motor to churn ice cream for 30 minutes or until motor starts to labor. (As ice melts and water drains off during churning, add more layers of ice and rock salt.) When churning is completed, drain off water from freezer tub. Let ice cream ripen for improved flavor and texture.

TO RIPEN:

Do not remove canister. Wipe canister lid and remove carefully so brine does not get into ice cream. Remove dasher; scrape off ice cream; pack down in canister. Cover canister with double thickness of waxed paper and replace lid; plug hole in lid. Repack freezer tub with alternate layers of ice and rock salt (4 parts ice to 1 part rock salt). Cover freezer with newspaper or heavy cloth. Be certain drainage holes in freezer are open. Let ice cream stand 1 hour to ripen.

NOTE: Store leftover ice cream in plastic freezer containers; place in home freezer. This dessert is a sure labor of love. The whole procedure can be done in advance, but half the fun is getting everyone to give a helping hand to churn the freezer!

LEO: JULY 23 to AUGUST 22

Exotic Diet

LIKE THE LION who rules your sign, you want to be king of the table as well as the jungle and the sky!

Being the host or hostess with the mostest is literally your scene since you're flamboyant, masterful, courageous, passionate, and, above all, generous. You can turn on the shyest, most reserved guests. But be careful you don't overdo it by coming on too strong or you will turn off people by your complete frankness and lack of self-restraint.

You adore entertaining friends and family on Sundays. You're happiest in the company of Arieans or Sagittarians. You love food that, like yourself, is colorful, dramatic, and exotic, appealing strongly to your keen sense of smell, sight, and taste. Not only do you cook with fire, but you like to perform, showing off your ability with dishes like flambé desserts or flaming steaks.

Since food for you is sensuous as well as entertaining, you seldom have turndowns to your invitations. One word of caution, though: since your appetite is larger than life, use moderation to avoid seeming ostentatious. Typically, you are strong and healthy and recuperate quickly from all illnesses. However, in later years, you are prone to have heart conditions and rheumatism. Keep yourself in top form!

FIRST DECAN: JULY 23 to AUGUST 2

Since Leos are ruled by the sun, they love grand and glorious menus! Leos entertain frequently and lavishly. They have a real thing about the tropics and love nothing better than to eat chicken dishes from south of the border or hot curries from far-off India!

For everyday dining, don't forget iron-rich beef, liver, and other blood-generating proteins so vital for Leos. Steak, chops and rare viands are in great demand. Leo's astrological foods are wide-ranging and fascinating—rice,* the versatile solar grain, stars in Stroganoff, curries, and salads.

Herbs (bay leaf * and rosemary *) and spices work well with food to turn the most banal fare into exotic, taste-tempting dishes. Walnuts,* poppy seeds,* and sunflower seeds * give interesting touches if used in salads, breads, or confections. Luckily, Leos' food range is probably the widest of all. There is very little they cannot take in stride and enjoy with gusto.

———

CALCUTTA CURRY *

Parslied Rice   Solar Curry Accompaniments *

Honey Custard * or Leonian Orange Date Cake *

Iced Coffee or Wine Cooler

-or-

COOL CUCUMBER YOGURT SOUP *

Skewered Beef *

Poppy Seed * Roll   Pungent Kale *

Apple Prune Betty *

CALCUTTA CURRY

3 *tbsps. butter or*   1½ *cups half and half or*
margarine   *light cream*
¼ *cup chopped onion*   2 *tbsps. cornstarch*
¼ *cup chopped celery*   ¼ *cup water*
1 *(2½-oz.) can sliced*   1 *(6-oz.) pkg. frozen*
mushrooms, drained   *Alaska king crab, thawed*
1½ *tsps. curry powder*   *hot cooked rice* *
½ *tsp. sea salt*   *choice of your favorite*
2 *tbsps. apple juice*   *accompaniments*
¼ *cup chicken broth*

Melt butter or margarine in saucepan. Cook onion, celery, mushrooms, curry powder, and salt in butter or margarine until onion is soft. Add apple juice, chicken broth, and half and half. Simmer slowly 5 minutes, stirring. Combine cornstarch and water; mix well. Stir into curry mixture. Cook over medium heat about 5 minutes or until thickened, stirring constantly. Stir in crab and heat through. Serve over hot cooked rice. Garnish with your choice of favorite accompaniments. Serve 4 to 5.

NOTE: Half the fun of hosting a Leonian bash is the pomp and circumstance that accompanies the meal! Calcutta curry is a perfect way to incorporate all of the lion's or lioness's astrological foods. For a delightfully different version of rice to complement the crab, cook 1 cup brown rice in 2½ cups salted boiling water about 45 minutes or until tender. Flavor with 1 cup chopped scallions, 1 cup shredded carrots cooked in 2 tbsps. corn oil; season with 3 tbsps. soy sauce and freshly ground black pepper.

SOLAR CURRY ACCOMPANIMENTS

Just dig in and throw the accompaniments on the side or on top of the curry. Improvisation on an astrological food list is just the beginning! Choose from:

GREENS: Cool, crisp cleaned lettuce, watercress, dandelion greens, or field lettuce.

CHUTNEY: Homemade fresh or top-quality bottled will do. Mango chutney is best on seafood or chicken curry; fresh fruit chutney such as solar mint chutney * or apricot orange * chutney can be made ahead.

FRUITS: Mandarin oranges,* grated coconut mixed with candied ginger *or* chopped fresh nectarines, cashews or walnuts flavored with a few drops fresh lemon * or lime juice, chopped chives and ground cinnamon *or* shredded cabbage, pineapple chunks (water-packed, drained), peanuts, and white pepper.

NUTS: Sunflower seeds,* butter-fried or oven-toasted; *or* peanuts, cashews, macadamias, walnuts,* pine nuts, pistachios or slivered almonds.

SOLAR MINT CHUTNEY *

2 cups fresh mint leaves
1 tbsp. chopped onion
2 canned chili peppers or
Tabasco to taste
¼ cup water
½ tsp. ground sage

½ tsp. sea salt
1 tbsp. honey
2 tbsps. fresh lemon juice *
½ tsp. finely grated lemon
peel *

Wash mint and place in blender container with onions, chili peppers, and water. Blend at high speed, stopping and stirring to blend evenly. Add remaining ingredients; blend a few minutes longer. Makes 1 cup.

APRICOT ORANGE * CHUTNEY

¾ cup California dried
  apricots, finely chopped
¼ cup water
¼ cup honey
½ cup tart apples, finely
  diced
½ cup seedless orange
  pulp *
¼ cup chopped walnuts *
1 tbsp. onion, minced
2 tbsps. fresh orange * or
  lemon * juice

¼ tsp. ground cinnamon *
⅛ tsp. ground nutmeg *
¼ cup freshly grated
  coconut or packaged,
  shredded coconut
3 drops Tabasco
½ tsp. orange or lemon
  rind,* finely grated

Combine apricots, water, and honey in saucepan; cover, bring to boil. Reduce heat, simmer 2 minutes or until water is absorbed. Stir frequently; cool. Combine cooled apricots with remaining ingredients. Let stand at room temperature at least 1 hour before serving. Makes about 1½ cups.

HONEY CUSTARD

2½ cups milk
4 eggs, slightly beaten
½ cup honey

1 tsp. pure vanilla extract
½ tsp. ground cinnamon *
dash sea salt

Scald milk. Blend eggs with honey; gradually stir in milk, vanilla, cinnamon, and salt. Pour into 6 custard cups. Place cups in pan with hot water. Bake in preheated 350° F. oven 30 minutes or until silver knife inserted in center comes out clean. Serve warm or well chilled, topped with sweetened strawberries. Serves 6.

LEONIAN ORANGE * DATE CAKE

1 cup butter
2 cups sugar
4 eggs
4 cups unbleached flour
1 tsp. baking soda
¼ tsp. sea salt
1⅓ cups buttermilk

1 pkg. (8 oz.) dates,
  chopped
1 cup chopped walnuts *
2 tsps. grated orange rind *
2 cups confectioners' sugar
1 cup orange juice *

Cream butter and sugar until light and fluffy. Add eggs one at a time, beating thoroughly after each addition. Add flour, sifted with soda and salt, in thirds alternately with buttermilk. Beat smooth after each addition. Fold in dates, nuts, and orange rind. Pour batter into a well-greased, floured 10-inch tube pan. Bake in preheated 325° F. oven 1½ hours. Blend confectioners' sugar with orange until dissolved. Pour icing over cake when removed from oven. Remove cake from pan when cool. Serves 16.

COOL CUCUMBER YOGURT SOUP

2 cups plain yogurt
1 cucumber, pared and
  diced
¾ tsp. sea salt

⅛ tsp. white pepper
1 to 2 tbsps. honey
2 tbsps. chopped walnuts *
  or pecans

Combine yogurt, cucumber, salt, and pepper in electric blender. Whirl until puréed and blended. Add honey to taste. Add 2 tbsps. walnuts * and whirl briefly. Chill thoroughly. Sprinkle each serving with additional chopped walnuts * if desired. Serves 6.

NOTE: One cup plain yogurt (made from partially skimmed milk) provides more than ¼ of the U.S. recommended daily allowance of calcium. Particularly great for adults who find it difficult to drink their calcium in the form of milk!

SKEWERED BEEF

2 lbs. *lean top-grade steak,* ¼ *cup fresh lemon juice*
 cut in 1-inch cubes *or wine vinegar*
1 lb. *large, fresh* ¼ *cup vegetable oil*
 mushrooms, washed ½ *bay leaf, crumbled*
⅓ *cup soy sauce*

Skewer beef alternately with mushrooms. Mix together soy sauce, lemon juice, oil, and bay leaf.* Marinate in soy-oil mixture several hours. Broil quickly, turning once, or grill over coals until golden. Baste while broiling. Serves 6 to 8.

PUNGENT KALE

1 *large bunch kale* 2 *tbsps. vegetable oil*
1 *large yellow onion,* 1 *tbsp. prepared yellow*
 peeled, sliced *mustard*
1 *clove garlic, pressed*

Wash kale, remove from stalk. Chop coarsely, save stalks for stock. Steam until tender, about 25 minutes. Meanwhile, sauté onion and garlic in oil. Add kale to onion and stir in mustard. Serves 4 to 6.

AFTERTHOUGHTS: Great to serve with cooked ham hocks or ham bone (cook with kale to flavor stock).

APPLE PRUNE BETTY

2 cups prunes, cooked	¼ cup margarine
2 apples	1 tsp. cinnamon *
3 cups soft bread crumbs or	½ tsp. nutmeg *
rolled oats	⅓ cup prune juice
⅓ cup raw sugar or honey	(or more)

Pit and cut prunes into small pieces. Pare, core and slice apples. Arrange 1 cup bread crumbs in bottom of well-greased baking dish. Cover with half the prunes, apples, sugar (or honey), cinnamon, and nutmeg. Repeat with another layer of crumbs and cover with remaining fruits and seasonings. Top with remaining crumbs. Pour prune juice over all. Cover, bake 1 hour in preheated oven 375° F. 1 hour. Serves 8.

AFTERTHOUGHTS: A pleasant inexpensive dessert starring two astrological foods for Leos (nutmeg * and cinnamon *).

SECOND DECAN: AUGUST 3 to AUGUST 12

Add to the sun the qualities of Jupiter and you are Leo at your best! You're optimistic, genial, and on the best of terms with your friends—even your foes! But because you're extravagant and willing to take risks, your grocery bills may exceed your food budget.

Moonlight and outdoor bashing are your style. Champagne suppers shared with your loved one are memorable when the menu stars delectable tidbits of food: fresh garden-ripe fruits, assorted cheeses, baked ham, cold pâté, or duck. While these foods appeal enormously to your exquisite palate, you can be happy with less elaborate menus featuring Leonian sirloin steak or Stroganoff stew. Planetary foods to please Jovian cooks include mushrooms,* peas,* asparagus,* endive,* currants,* dandelion greens,* jasmine tea,* rose hips,* sage,* and chervil.*

STROGANOFF STEW * OR SIRLOIN STEAK LEONIAN *

Asparagus with Parsley Sauce *

Cherry Tomato Bake in Sage Butter Sauce

Poppy Seed Rolls

Endive * Salad with French Dressing
or Dandelion Salad

Nectarine-Cherry Coupe Flambé *

Jasmine Tea *

STROGANOFF STEW

2½ lbs. lean boneless
    round, cut in 1½-inch
    cubes
3 tbsps. oil
½ lb. sliced fresh
    mushrooms *
3 tbsps. unbleached flour
2½ cups boiling water
¼ cup instant minced onion

¼ tsp. instant minced
    garlic
1 beef bouillon cube
2 tbsps. original
    Worcestershire sauce
1 tsp. sea salt
1 cup dairy sour cream
2 tbsps. tomato paste
2 tbsps. chopped fresh
    parsley

Trim excess fat from meat, discard. Heat oil in a Dutch oven. Add meat, brown on all sides. Remove meat, set aside. Add mushrooms, sauté 5 minutes. Stir in flour; cook 2 minutes longer. Gradually stir in water. Add onion, garlic, bouillon cube, 1 tbsp. Worcestershire sauce, salt, and reserved meat. Cover, reduce heat and simmer 1½ hours or until meat is tender. Combine sour cream, tomato paste, and remaining Worcestershire sauce, stir into meat. Heat, but do not boil. Stir in parsley. Serve over cooked broad noodles if desired. Serves 6.

SIRLOIN STEAK LEONIAN

2 tbsps. crushed
  peppercorns
1 steak: sirloin or London
  broil, cut 2 inches thick,
  weighing about 4 lbs.
½ tsp. sea salt

½ cup butter or margarine
2 tbsps. fine-grade olive oil
⅓ cup dry white wine
⅓ cup beef broth
3 tbsps. cognac or brandy
chopped parsley or chives

Firmly press crushed pepper into both sides of steak using heel of hand. Sprinkle salt on both sides of steak. Melt butter or margarine over high heat in heavy, cast-iron skillet, large enough to hold steak. When butter-oil mixture is sizzling, sear steak quickly on both sides. Cook steak over medium heat about 4 minutes per side for rare, 5 minutes for medium-rare, 6–7 minutes for well done. Remove steak to heated platter. Add wine and broth to pan juices. Bring to boil, stirring. Lower heat. Heat cognac or brandy; spoon over steak and ignite. Spoon sauce over steak. Garnish with parsley or chives. Serves 6.

AFTERTHOUGHTS: Leonians adore the pomp and circumstance of this dish! Ignite and serve table-side. For an unusual taste, add a twist of lemon rind to sauce as it cooks down. Remove before serving. All Leonians and guests will be in extreme harmony!

ASPARAGUS * WITH PARSLEY SAUCE

2 tbsps. butter or
margarine
2 tbsps. unbleached flour
1 cup chicken stock
½ cup light cream
¾ tsp. sea salt

⅛ tsp. freshly ground
black pepper
2 large egg yolks
1 tbsp. snipped fresh
parsley
2½ lbs. fresh cooked
asparagus *

Melt butter or margarine in saucepan. Remove from heat, blend in flour. Stir in chicken stock (or 1 chicken bouillon cube dissolved in 1 cup boiling water) and ¼ cup of the cream. Return to heat; stir and cook over low heat until mixture thickens, about 5 minutes. Add salt and pepper. Beat egg yolks, mix with remaining cream. Stir into sauce. Serve over hot cooked asparagus. Serves 6.

NOTE: Asparagus, ruled by Jupiter, is often thought of as an aphrodisiac!

NECTARINE-CHERRY COUPE FLAMBÉ

2 or 3 fresh California
    nectarines
¼ cup honey
1½ tbsps. cornstarch
¼ tsp. sea salt
1 tsp. grated lemon rind
1 can (12 fluid oz.) cherry
    cola
4 drops red food coloring

1 tbsp. lemon juice
few dashes aromatic bitters,
    optional
1 cup pitted fresh
    Bing cherries or
    canned red cherries,
    pitted
1 tbsp. Chartreuse,
    optional
1 quart vanilla ice cream

Slice nectarines to yield 1½ cups. Combine honey, cornstarch, salt, and lemon rind in saucepan. Stir in cherry cola and heat, stirring over medium heat until mixture comes to a boil, thickens, and clears. Stir in food color, lemon juice, bitters, nectarines, and cherries; heat through. Set Chartreuse aflame, pour over hot fruit sauce. Stir, serve over scoops of vanilla ice cream.

JASMINE TEA

2 qts. boiling water
¼ cup loose jasmine tea *

2 lemon or orange rinds,
    grated
scant cup honey

Pour boiling water over tea, lemon or orange rind. Cover, let stand 5 minutes. Strain into hot teapot, add honey, stir to dissolve. Serves 10.

THIRD DECAN: AUGUST 13 to AUGUST 22

Add to the sun the qualities of Mercury and you become your most eloquent, quick-witted self, making you the most dazzling host or hostess on the planet. During these long, lazy summer days, your guests are dazzled by your devastating charm and easygoing manner! Quick, last-minute meals show off your cooking prowess, but you're more inclined to hang in there despite the mercury's climb. At times, you seem restless, talkative, and nervous. Be sure to keep your mind on your cooking.

You have a ball creating lovely summer brunches to consume in the patio or garden. And by now you're tawny and tanned like a lion from being outdoors during the brightest summer days.

CHICKEN AZTEC *

Rice and Carrot Ring *   Green Beans, French Style

Savory-Dilled * Tomatoes

Banana Frost and Fire *

Iced Coffee

-or-

LEONIAN MIDSUMMER BRUNCH IN THE GARDEN

Merry-Go-Round Fruits *

Chived Eggs Scramble   Grilled Italian Sausages

Toasted English Muffins   Sun God Coffee Cake *

Brunch Punch *

CHICKEN AZTEC

1 *broiler-fryer chicken,*
  cut in 8 pieces or *4*
  chicken breasts
¼ *cup butter or margarine*
2 *cups hot water*
2 *tbsps. minced chives*
2 *tsps. sea salt*
⅛ *tsp. freshly ground*
  black pepper
¼ *cup cornstarch*

¼ *cup cold water*
½ *cup pitted ripe olives,*
  chopped
½ *cup diced green pepper*
1 *tbsp. chopped pimiento*
1 *tbsp. fresh lemon juice*
½ *tsp. crushed rosemary* *
2 *California avocados*
½ *square unsweetened*
  chocolate, grated

Brown chicken in melted butter or margarine; add hot water, chives, salt, and pepper. Cover. Cook over medium heat 35 minutes or until chicken is tender. Reserve broth, add enough water to make 2 cups. Cut chicken into bite-sized pieces.

Combine cornstarch and cold water; add to chicken broth. Cook over low heat, stirring constantly until mixture is thickened. Add chicken, olives, green pepper, pimiento, lemon juice, and rosemary. Cook over low heat about 6 minutes or until green pepper is tender. Cut avocados lengthwise into halves; remove pits and skin. Cut fruit into balls with melon ball cutter or ½ teaspoon measure. Stir into hot chicken mixture with sherry and chocolate. Place over low heat, stirring gently until chocolate melts. Serves 4.

NOTE: This Leonian specialty was inspired by ancient Aztec Indians who worshiped the sun and consumed vast quantities of avocados in their daily diet.

Rosemary, * the solar herb, takes its name from the sea, meaning "dew of the sea." According to legend, the pungent herb "restored the mind, averted the evil eye"! Rosemary has been valued for its symbolism and heavenly scent as well as for its medicinal and culinary uses. Ecologists please note: it protects neighboring plants and orchard trees from insects. During the 17th century it was burned by French nurses to purify the air. European gypsies brewed a concoction of the aromatic herb called "Queen of Hungary's water," and peddled it all over the world as a cure-all and beautifier.

Rosemary has been used by ancient doctors not only as a brain stimulant but as a remedy for heart trouble. (Remember, even the strong-hearted Leonians must watch out for heart strain.) Above all, rosemary does enchanting things to food, particularly fowl, beef, or fish.

RICE AND CARROT * RING

3 cups cooked rice	1 can (10½ oz.) cheese
2 cups fresh carrots,* grated	soup, undiluted
	1 egg, slightly beaten
½ cup onion, grated	1 tsp. sea salt
2 tbsps. unbleached flour	¼ tsp. ground white pepper
	1 tsp. Worcestershire sauce
	dash of Tabasco

Combine rice, carrots, onion, and flour. Blend soup, egg, and seasonings; add to rice mixture. Pour into well-greased 8-inch ring mold. Bake in preheated 350° F. oven 30 minutes. Cool 10 minutes before turning out on serving plate. Serve with green vegetables, preferably green beans. Serves 6.

NOTE: A lovely way to combine rice, the solar grain, with colorful carrots and subtle cheese!

BANANA FROST AND FIRE

2 *quarts chocolate ice*	1 *tsp. cream of tartar*
cream	1 *cup sugar*
5 *large bananas*	2 *tbsps. rum (150-proof)*
8 *egg whites*	

Pack ice cream into a deep 6-cup glass bowl. Cover, freeze until firm. Unmold ice cream onto cold board. Peel 4 bananas, cut in half lengthwise and again into halves crosswise. Press bananas into ice cream. Peel remaining banana, cut into slices, pile on top of mold. Place in freezer while preparing meringue. Beat egg whites with cream of tartar until soft peaks form. Gradually beat in sugar; continue beating until egg whites become very stiff, about 15 minutes. Remove ice cream from freezer, spread meringue over bananas and ice cream, making sure meringue completely covers all. Make a well 1 inch deep in top of meringue. Bake in preheated 450° F. oven 3 minutes, or until meringue is slightly golden. Heat rum, pour into well in top of meringue, ignite. Serve at once. Serves 10.

NOTE: A dramatic production and beautiful to taste!

MERRY-GO-ROUND FRUITS

*3 fresh California
   nectarines
⅓ cup honey
¼ tsp. ground ginger
dash sea salt
⅔ cup water
⅓ cup sauterne wine or
   2 tbsps. fresh lemon juice*

*1 cup strawberries,
   halved, or whole
   raspberries
½ cup blueberries
½ cup fresh melon balls
   (cantaloupe or
   honeydew melon)
mint sprigs*

Slice nectarines into wide-mouth quart jar. Blend honey, ginger, and salt in saucepan. Add water, bring to boil. Pour over nectarines; add wine. Cover, chill several hours or overnight. Turn into bowl; add remaining fruits. Garnish with mint. Serves 4 to 6.

SUN GOD COFFEE CAKE

For the filling:

4 or 5 large fresh
  California nectarines
1 tbsp. fresh lemon * juice
¾ cup honey

½ tsp. ground cinnamon
2 tbsps. cornstarch
2 tbsps. butter or
  margarine

Slice nectarines to measure 4 cups. Place in saucepan; add lemon juice.* Mix honey, cinnamon and cornstarch; sprinkle over nectarines. Cook over low heat, stirring constantly until mixture thickens and comes to a boil. Remove from heat; add butter or margarine. Cool; set aside.

For the coffee cake:

½ cup half and half
1 pkg. dry active yeast
⅓ cup butter or margarine
⅓ cup honey
1 tsp. grated lemon rind

2 eggs
2⅓ cups unbleached flour
1 tsp. sea salt
nectarine filling

Scald half and half; cool slightly. Sprinkle yeast over cream; stir well to dissolve yeast. Cream butter or margarine, honey, and lemon rind until light and fluffy. Beat in eggs. Sift flour with salt; reserve ⅓ cup. Add remainder to creamed mixture alternately with yeast mixture. Spread ¾ of dough into greased 9-inch-square pan. Cover with nectarine filling. Blend reserved flour with remaining dough; roll into 9-inch square. Cut into strips about ¾ inch wide. Arrange lattice-fashion over filling. Cover, let rise in warm place about 40 minutes. Bake in preheated 375° F. oven 25 to 30 minutes. Brush with melted butter. Serve warm. Serves 8.

BRUNCH PUNCH

3 fresh nectarines
6 eggs
3 cups milk
1 tbsp. honey

1½ tsps. instant
coffee powder
1 tsp. pure vanilla extract
dash salt
soft ice cream

Slice nectarine, reserving 6 slices for each garnish. Whir in blender or mash; beat with all remaining ingredients except ice cream. Pour into 6 tall glasses. Add ice cream. Garnish each glass with nectarine slices. Serves 6.

VIRGO: AUGUST 23 to SEPTEMBER 22

A Born Planner!

YOUR OUTWARD APPEARANCE and behavior can be very deceiving! Inwardly you are introspective and sometimes indecisive. You're super careful about your diet, often becoming a vegetarian. In general, you seem to need less food than people born under other signs.

Your patience and your love of children make you an excellent nurse, willing to prepare special food to see them through illnesses. And your great memory makes you able to reel off a recipe you tried only once ages ago!

Your only real hangup is being able to please yourself. You're a born perfectionist and planner. You work tirelessly to create an orderly, harmonious environment, especially in the home. Typically your patterns have been set early in life. You thrive on routine even when it comes to marketing and preparing meals.

The social scene is not for you and yet you love being invited to parties because you're a people-watcher. You are usually an extraordinarily good cook striving hard to please your family. Choose Wednesdays to entertain your friends at small family-type dinners at home. You're happiest in the company of Capricornians or Taureans.

FIRST DECAN: AUGUST 23 to SEPTEMBER 2

Since you are ruled by Mercury, you are quick-witted, hungry for knowledge, persevering but often restless and, at times, too presumptuous in your judgments. You prefer a general diet with a wide variety, ranging from all kinds of meats (in limited quantity) to vegetables and cereals daily at different meals.

Typically, you're a start-from-scratch cook, turned on by baking homemade bread or cakes. Often you're a vegetarian, so rely on spices and herbs but only in nominal amounts. Milk, cheese and dairy products are terrific choices for you. You're a whiz with soufflés, omelets, soups, and salads!

You adore using your newest kitchen gadget. You're also practical and prefer buying natural foods rather than the more expensive foods in health food stores. You detest added girth and eat small portions. However, remember to keep meals hearty enough to satisfy the appetites of guests who need more food than you do. You have a green thumb and often grow your own herbs. Fennel,* parsley,* marjoram,* caraway,* savory,* and dill * are delightful herbs to perk up your diet. Since you're the spiritual type, you are far more interested in what food will do for your mind and soul than merely being fully integrated to the table.

Your daily routine should always begin with planned, nutritious breakfasts!

VIRGONIANS' BREAKFAST

Fresh Orange Juice   Familia * with Cream

Banana Flip *

- or -

Spiced Granola * with Blueberries

Crisp Bacon   Apple Juice

- or -

Sliced Oranges   Chive Omelet *

- or -

Peggy's Wheat Germ Breakfast Ringers *

Skimmed Milk

FAMILIA

3 cups quick oats   3 cups rolled wheat or
1½ cups wheat germ   wheat flakes
1 pkg. (8 oz.) dried   2 cups raisins
   apricots, cut up   1 cup raw sugar or honey
1 cup chopped nuts   1 yellow apple, chopped

Mix everything together except chopped apple. Store in
covered jars in refrigerator. Serve with chopped apples, milk,
and honey. Serves 12 to 15.

NOTE: Any dried fruits or nuts can be used. Any flaked grain
such as bran or rye will do. Familia is a terrific way to start the
day, particularly for vegetarians. Sliced banana and a dollop of
pineapple or orange yogurt makes a complete meal-in-one for
brunch or snack.

BANANA FLIP

1½ cups cold milk
2 tbsps. peanut butter

3 tbsps. wheat germ
1 banana, quartered

Put all ingredients in blender container. Cover, blend at high speed 30 seconds. Refrigerate ahead of time if desired. Makes 2¼ cups.

SPICED GRANOLA

4 cups old-fashioned
or quick oats
1 can (4 oz.) shredded
coconut
½ cup sesame seed
½ cup sunflower seed

½ cup toasted wheat germ
1½ tsps. ground cinnamon
1 tsp. ground nutmeg
½ cup honey
½ cup vegetable oil
1 cup dark raisins

Combine oats, coconut, sesame seed, sunflower seed, wheat germ, cinnamon, and nutmeg. Add honey and oil; mix well. Pour into two 15- × 10- × 1½-inch jelly-roll pans. Bake in a preheated 350° F. oven until golden, about 18 minutes, stirring often. Cool and crumble. Stir in raisins. Store in tightly covered containers. Mixture keeps best if refrigerated. Different and delicious for breakfast! Glorious used as topping over vanilla ice cream or lemon ice or pineapple sherbet for a crunchy, tasty finale to a meal! Makes about 10 cups.

CHIVE OMELET

3 eggs	*1 tsp. chopped parsley* *
1 tbsp. cold water	*sea salt, white pepper to*
1 tbsp. chopped chives	*taste*
	2 tbsps. butter

Beat eggs with cold water just long enough to blend. Stir in chives, parsley, salt, and pepper to taste. Melt butter in omelet pan; tilt pan in all directions over high heat. When butter is sizzling, pour in egg mixture. Shake pan over heat to lightly brown omelet bottom. Tilt pan over so omelet folds as it slips into dish. Sprinkle more chives over top for garnish. Serve immediately. Serves 1.

PEGGY'S WHEAT GERM BREAKFAST RINGERS

7 tbsps. butter	*2 hard-cooked egg*
2 tbsps. brown sugar,	*yolks, grated*
packed	*3 tbsps. milk*
¾ cup wheat germ	*Cinnamon topping* *
¾ cup unbleached flour	*(cinnamon and brown*
½ tsp. sea salt	*sugar)*

Beat 6 tbsps. butter with sugar until blended. Mix in wheat germ, flour, salt, and grated egg yolks. Blend in milk to form dough. Roll out on floured surface to 11-inch round. Cut with floured 2¾-inch doughnut cutter or fancy cooky cutter. Brush ringers and hole with 1 tbsp. melted butter and sprinkle with cinnamon topping. Place on ungreased baking sheet. Bake in preheated 350° F. oven 12 to 14 minutes or until golden brown on bottom. Remove from baking sheet. Cool on rack. Makes 15 to 18 ringers and holes.

NOTE: Great for breakfast or mid-morning coffee break. Loaded with the B vitamins!

SECOND DECAN: SEPTEMBER 3 to SEPTEMBER 12

To the qualities of Mercury add Saturn's influences: you are tactful, thrifty, stubborn with others as well as yourself! Now is the time when you love to whip up an omelet or soufflé for early fall Saturday brunches. Weekends are a terrific time to turn on appetites with homemade bread that comes wafting from your kitchen.

Due to your guru Saturnine qualities, you love one-dish meals featuring menus as tasteful and nutritious as a New England boiled dinner. You love plotting menus, looking through old recipe books, even on Saturday nights while your friends are out dancing.

VIRGONIAN NEW ENGLAND BOILED DINNER *

Savory Salad Toss *

Hot Saffron * Bread * or Rye and Oat Bread *

- or -

LUMPY VEGETABLE SOUP * or
SPICY CHEESE SOUFFLÉ *

Dill Marinated Vegetables *

Lemon Sherbert   Hazelnut Cake *

- or -

SAUTÉED LIVER AND VEGETABLE DINNER *

Italian Salad Toss *

Honey Apricot Snow *

Minted Ice Tea

VIRGONIAN NEW ENGLAND BOILED DINNER

1 corned brisket of beef,
weighing about 5 lbs.
1 onion, peeled, sliced
1 tbsp. whole cloves
6 peppercorns
1 small clove garlic, peeled
pinch rosemary
1 stalk celery, chopped

8 carrots, well scrubbed,
cut in large pieces
8 small potatoes, peeled
8 small onions, peeled
4 turnips,* peeled, cut in
pieces
1 large head cabbage, cut
in large wedges

Wipe brisket with damp cloth; put in large soup kettle. Add water to cover. Add sliced onion, cloves, peppercorns, garlic, rosemary, celery, and 1 cut-up carrot. Bring to boil, removing scum that forms on surface. Cover, simmer about 4 hours, or until tender. About 25 minutes before serving, add carrots, potatoes, onions, and turnips; simmer until tender. Add cabbage wedges; cook 7 minutes longer or until cabbage is barely tender. Slice meat; arrange on warm serving platter. Surround with vegetables. Serve 8 to 10.

SAVORY SALAD TOSS

4 cups crisp salad greens   *1 tsp. dill seed*
1 cup diced celery   *½ tsp. sea salt*
1 tsp. snipped fresh savory *   *freshly ground black*
(or use dried)   *pepper to taste*
½ cup dairy sour cream   *2 tsps. fresh lemon juice*
1 tbsp. chopped onion

Combine all ingredients. Toss lightly to blend. Serves 8.

HOT SAFFRON * BREAD

1 loaf French or Italian   *4 tbsps. soft butter*
bread   *pinch powdered saffron* *
*   1 sheet aluminum foil*

Slice loaf diagonally with sharp knife in thick slices without completely cutting through loaf. Cream together butter and saffron.* Spread each slice generously with saffron butter. Squeeze slices back together. Wrap tightly in aluminum foil. Heat 10 minutes in preheated 400° F. oven. Serves 3 or 4.

NOTE: The world's most expensive seasoning is very powerful in flavor. Use sparingly! This pungent herb, made from dried stigmas of the saffron crocus, is said to provoke laughter and merriment—great for glum Virgos—and used as medicine, dye, and condiment. Primarily imported from Spain, it comes from the Arabic word meaning "yellow." In ancient Rome, saffron was used to scent baths, theaters, and public places. Medieval physicians claimed saffron could banish all ailments from toothaches to plague! Used in Far East as tonic, stomachic, aphrodisiac.

RYE AND OAT BREAD

2 envelopes yeast	1 tbsp. sea salt
¼ cup lukewarm water	1 egg, beaten
⅓ cup dark molasses	½ cup oat flour
1 cup boiling water	3 cups rye flour
2 tbsps. butter	2 tbsps. caraway * seeds

Dissolve yeast in lukewarm water with molasses until frothy. Mix boiling water with butter and salt; cool to room temperature. Add beaten egg to yeast mixture. Mix together flours; add caraway * seeds. Combine liquid and flours; beat hard with wooden spoon until dough is elastic and smooth. Set mixing bowl in pan of warm water. Cover bowl, let dough rise until doubled in bulk. Punch down, let rise again until doubled in bulk. Turn out dough on lightly floured board. Shape loaf to fit a 3- × 5- × 9-inch bread pan. Put dough in greased bread pan. Cover, let rise until doubled in volume. Bake in preheated 400° F. oven 15 minutes. Reduce oven temperature to 325° F.; bake 40 minutes longer or until bread is done. Cool on cake rack; oil top lightly with butter to keep crust soft. Slice to serve warm or cold. Terrific spread with soft sweet butter or homemade apple butter. Marvelous toasted for breakfast with lemon-scented tea! Makes 1 loaf.

NOTE: Virgonians who eat for health reasons treasure old-fashioned recipes, particularly bread made with natural grains. Rye and oat bread is truly a winner! Caraway * seed, the aromatic herb, is a favorite herb of Virgonians!

LUMPY VEGETABLE SOUP

2 small peeled, cubed
  potatoes
3 peeled diced carrots *
3 stalks chopped celery
2 leeks or scallions, white
  part only, chopped
3 tbsps. vegetable oil
½ cup dry white wine or
  clam juice
1 zucchini, cut in large
  cubes
2 cups green beans,
  chopped
½ small cauliflower, cut
  into small flowerets
1 can (13¾ oz.) chicken
  broth

1 tbsp. chopped fresh
  marjoram * or chervil
  or 2 tsps. dried
1 tbsp. snipped
  fresh parsley *
1 bay leaf
1 tsp. sea salt
pinch of freshly ground
  black pepper
8 or more large lettuce
  leaves, broken
  into large pieces
1 cup freshly grated
  Parmesan or Romano
  cheese

Sauté potatoes, carrots, celery, and leeks in vegetable oil until barely tender, about 7 to 10 minutes. Add wine, cook uncovered over low heat until wine is almost evaporated. Add zucchini, green beans and cauliflower, chicken broth, marjoram, parsley, bay leaf, salt, and pepper. Bring to boil, cover. Simmer gently until vegetables are barely tender, about 10 minutes. Taste to correct seasonings. Add lettuce leaves and grated cheese. Allow cheese to melt before ladling soup into individual soup bowls. Delicious with pâté, cold fried chicken and fruit for dessert. Serves 4.

AFTERTHOUGHTS: Light, lovely, and crammed full of vitamins! To make it heartier, serve with strips of leftover white meat of turkey or chicken!

SPICY CHEESE SOUFFLÉ

½ *cup tomato juice*
1 tsp. original
Worcestershire sauce
½ *tsp. sea salt*
1 tsp. summer savory *
⅓ *cup butter*

3 tbsps. unbleached flour
1 cup grated sharp
Cheddar cheese
½ *tsp. dry mustard*
4 eggs, divided
white pepper to taste

Heat tomato juice, Worcestershire sauce, salt, and summer savory in small saucepan. Simmer 10 minutes; strain. Melt butter in another saucepan; blend in flour, stirring constantly. Add tomato juice mixture, stirring. Cook until thick and smooth, stirring occasionally. Stir in cheese and mustard; blend well. Cool cheese-tomato mixture. Beat egg yolks; blend into cheese-tomato mixture. Beat egg whites until stiff but not dry. Fold them into cheese mixture carefully. Add white pepper to taste; blend well. Pour into an unbuttered 1½-quart soufflé dish. Bake in preheated 325° F. oven 35 minutes. Serve at once. Serves 4.

NOTE: Savory, the pungent Virgonian herb, is supposed to be the chosen herb of satyrs; that's probably why it was renowned as an aphrodisiac!

DILL MARINATED VEGETABLES

1 pkg. (10 oz.) frozen cauliflower	1 tsp. dill seed *
1 pkg. (9 oz.) frozen sliced green beans	½ tsp. instant minced garlic
2 tbsps. olive oil	½ tsp. sea salt
2 tbsps. wine vinegar	1/16 tsp. freshly ground black pepper
	½ cup crisp bacon, crumbled

Cook vegetables according to package directions. Drain. Combine oil, vinegar, dill seed, garlic, salt, and black pepper. Pour over cauliflower and beans. Toss gently. Serve either hot or cold, garnished with crisp bacon bits. Serves 6.

NOTE: In days gone by, dill, ruled by Mercury, was considered black magic! With dill seeds and the right incantation, a hip witch could make an enemy's cake fall, take the curl out of her hair, or give the family cat a fit of sneezes! With dill seeds, one can cure hiccups and headaches, relieve itching, indigestion, and insomnia. Dill is thought to come from a Norwegian word meaning to quiet or soothe.

HAZELNUT * CAKE

1 cup butter	1 cup milk
2 cups raw sugar	1 tsp. pure vanilla extract
4 eggs	1 cup ground hazelnuts *
3 cups sifted unbleached	or black walnuts
flour	confectioners' sugar
1 tbsp. baking powder	

Grease 9-inch tube pan; line bottom with aluminum foil. Cream butter; gradually add sugar, beating until light and fluffy. Add eggs one at a time, beating well after each addition. Sift together dry ingredients; fold in alternately with milk and vanilla. Fold in nuts. Spoon into tube pan. Bake in preheated 350° F. 1¼ hours or until done. Cool in pan. Remove from pan. Sift confectioners' sugar over top. Serves 12 to 16.

NOTE: Hazelnuts are a Virgonian delight but are sometimes difficult to obtain. This old-fashioned version of pound cake came from an old German family. The cake improves in flavor and texture if stored several days in a tightly covered container.

SAUTÉED LIVER AND VEGETABLE DINNER

1 lb. beef liver, sliced
(about 4 pieces)
2 tbsps. unbleached flour
⅓ cup margarine
2 cups sliced fresh
mushrooms
1 large green or red
pepper, cut in rings

4 medium-sized tomatoes,
peeled and diced
1 small tender zucchini,
cut in rounds
1½ tsps. sea salt
dash of paprika
½ tsp. chili powder
½ lemon
1 tbsp. chopped chives

Dip liver in flour; shake off excess flour. Melt margarine in large skillet until sizzling. Cook liver quickly in margarine until brown on both sides. Stir in remaining ingredients except lemon. Heat to boiling. Reduce heat; simmer covered until liver and vegetables are tender. Do not overcook. Sprinkle with lemon juice and chives. Serves 4.

ITALIAN SALAD TOSS

1 clove garlic, cut
1 head crisp, cleaned
lettuce or mixed greens,
about 2 qts.
2 Italian plum tomatoes,
cut in wedges
½ green pepper, cut in
strips

6 radishes, sliced
1 small red onion, peeled
and thinly sliced
1 cup seasoned croutons
favorite bottled Italian
dressing

Rub salad bowl with garlic. Add lettuce or greens. Arrange remaining ingredients over top. Toss lightly with Italian dressing. Serve at once. Serves 4 to 6.

NOTE: A dieter's delight if low-calorie dressing is used. Fresh herbs (dill, parsley, or basil) make delightful taste additions.

HONEY APRICOT SNOW

1 envelope unflavored gelatin	*1 container (8 oz.) apricot yogurt*
½ cup cold water	*1 tbsp. fresh lemon juice*
½ tsp. ginger	*3 egg whites*
⅛ tsp. sea salt	*¼ cup honey*

Sprinkle gelatin over cold water in saucepan. Place over low heat; stir constantly until gelatin dissolves. Remove from heat; stir in ginger and salt. Blend in yogurt and lemon juice. Chill, stirring often until slightly thickened. Beat egg whites until soft peaks form; gradually add honey and beat until very stiff peaks form. Fold in gelatin-yogurt mixture. Turn into 4-cup mold or individual dishes. Chill until set. Serve very cold. Wonderful with stirred custard sauce! Serves 6 to 8.

THIRD DECAN: SEPTEMBER 13 to SEPTEMBER 22

Add the qualities of Venus to Mercury, and you are your most romantic self! You seek beautifully serene settings for meals, often served outdoors to capture and enjoy the lingering warmth of Indian summer.

While stressing the harmony of carefully planned meals to feature color contrasts and pleasing flavor nuances, you appear to be outwardly cheerful. However, you have a tendency to act introverted, postponing important decisions and being self-indulgent and slightly extravagant. Choose your dinner guests carefully. You aren't quite tuned in to the social scene, as your mind seems to be in another time and place!

The beautiful fall harvest of Venusian fruits adds color as well as flavor to provide the finale to your meals.

QUICHE LORRAINE *

Celestial Green Beans *

Herbed Sliced Tomatoes

Fall Fruit Tray: Apples,* Pears,* Peaches,* and Grapes *

- or -

DILLED HALIBUT AND CUCUMBER SALAD *

Lima Bean *-Corn Succotash

Italian Breadsticks   Butter Curls

Apple * Pie Bake *

QUICHE LORRAINE

1 10-inch prepared pie crust	*1 egg yolk*
¼ cup onion, minced	*2½ cups light cream*
1½ tbsps. butter	*⅛ tsp. ground nutmeg*
1 cup crisp bacon crumbles, or diced, cooked smoked ham	*½ tsp. sea salt*
	dash ground cayenne
	⅛ tsp. white pepper
5 eggs	*1 cup grated Swiss or Gruyère cheese*

Line a deep 10-inch pie pan with prepared pastry. Prick shell, partially bake in preheated 400° F. oven 8 to 9 minutes or until shell starts to brown. Remove crust from oven; set aside. Cook onion in butter until soft. Mix onion-butter mixture with bacon or ham. Beat together eggs and egg yolk until light. Add cream, nutmeg, salt, cayenne, and white pepper, blend well. Put meat-onion mixture in shell; top with grated cheese. Pour custard over all. Sprinkle top with ground nutmeg. Bake in preheated 375° F. oven 30 to 35 minutes until filling is golden and puffy, or until a knife inserted into the center comes out clean. Serve hot, at room temperature, or cold. Terrific as a main course or for hors d'oeuvres, cut into small pieces or baked in individual tart or muffin tins. Serves 4 to 6.

AFTERTHOUGHTS: Quiche Lorraine, a favorite from France, is now becoming a standard American fare. The delicate custard—aromatic with a hint of spices and the mildest nuances of onion and bacon or ham—makes it astrologically and temperamentally perfect for Virgonians who like to eat lightly but carefully.

CELESTIAL GREEN BEANS *

*1 pkg. frozen green beans **
2 tbsps. butter
½ tsp. dried savory
sea salt

freshly ground black pepper
1 tsp. fresh lemon juice
½ tsp. finely grated lemon rind

Cook beans according to package instructions. Melt butter; toss over hot drained beans. Add savory and salt and pepper to taste; toss lightly with lemon juice and rind. Serve piping hot. Serves 4.

DILLED HALIBUT AND CUCUMBER SALAD

1 pkg. (12 oz.) frozen halibut steaks
1 tbsp. instant minced onion
1 tbsp. water
1 tbsp. dill seed

½ tsp. sea salt
⅛ tsp. ground white pepper
½ cup dairy sour cream
1 tbsp. lemon juice
1 large cucumber, peeled, thinly sliced

Simmer fish in water to cover until done (about 10 minutes). Cool. Remove bones and skin. Cut fish into small chunks; set aside. Mix onion with water; let stand 10 minutes to soften. Combine onion, dill, salt, white pepper, sour cream, and lemon juice in salad bowl. Mix well. Add fish and cucumber. Toss gently, coating with sour cream mixture. Serves 6.

NOTE: A delightful dish to serve finicky Virgos! Dill, ruled by Mercury, is a terrific "brain food," used by medieval doctors to improve nerves, nails, and hair and quiet colicky babies.

APPLE * PIE BAKE

2 prepared pie crusts
(homemade or prepared
according to pkg.
instructions)
about 2½ lbs. tart green
apples *

4 tbsps. honey
2 tsps. fresh lemon juice
few dashes sea salt
½ tsp. ground cinnamon
or mace
2 tbsps. butter

Prepare lower crust to line a deep 9-inch pie dish. Wash, core, slice apples into thin slices. Leave skins on. Drizzle honey over apples; add lemon juice, salt, cinnamon or mace. Toss to coat apples. Pile apple mixture into baking dish. Dot with butter. Top with upper crust. Crimp crusts together to seal. Bake in preheated 400° F. oven about 45 minutes. Cool to room temperature. Serves 6.

AFTERTHOUGHTS: For pleasant nutritious variations mix apple slices with sesame seeds, chopped nuts, peaches, or berries. Serve with hunk of good aged Cheddar or a dollop of yogurt.

LIBRA: SEPTEMBER 23 to OCTOBER 22

Subtle and Sumptuous!

SINCE YOURS IS an air sign, you're a dreamer, romanticist (you're ruled by Venus) and idealist.

You much prefer planning and preparing meals to doing the kitchen cleanup! Monday is the happiest day for you to up to your dreams and schemes, since it means coming to grips with the realities of life. You enjoy taking your time when you look at a menu. Taking your pick from the buffet table turns you on.

You have a great need for privacy, and enjoy dining in quiet romantic settings. You have tremendous appreciation for beautifully prepared foods, and almost gourmet tastes because you prefer simply prepared fare made with fresh ingredients, subtly flavored.

You much prefer planning and preparing meals to doing the kitchen cleanup! Monday is the happiest day for you to entertain. Normally, you are healthy, but look out for kidney flare-ups. You are better off keeping busy doing things you enjoy.

FIRST DECAN: SEPTEMBER 23 to OCTOBER 2

You have a passion for haute cuisine. Everything you eat and serve must be expertly prepared, elegantly served. You pay as much attention to an artistically set table with gorgeous china and cutlery as you do the food itself!

When dining out you seek top-notch restaurants and judge for yourself; you don't depend on restaurant critics. At home you like to uphold the same high standard. Your downfall may be your sweet tooth, especially rich pastries made with the lovely Venusian fruits of autumn.

You need quantities of milk, fruits, and vegetables to keep healthy. Eat meat sparingly, and substitute fish and fowl to get essential proteins to sustain life. Since your dominant trait is balance, there is little you can't eat as long as you use reason and consume moderate amounts. Drink quantities of fresh fruit juice, abstaining almost entirely from alcoholic beverages. Luckily for you, your astrological list is long and lovely: wheat, sorrel, plums, catnip,* mint,* thyme,* chestnuts,* beans,* pears,* apples,* peaches,* raspberries,* and grapes.*

Choose your dinner partners carefully. You are compatible with other Librans, Aquarians, and Geminians. Keep menus simple but still gourmet by starring subtle foods! Keep the guest list short!

LEMON BROILED CHICKEN VENUSIAN *

Carrot Lemon Pilaf *   Minted * Peas *

Mixed Green Salad

Peach * of a Pie *

Catnip * Tea

LEMON BROILED CHICKEN VENUSIAN

*1½ lbs. boneless
  chicken breasts
1 lemon, squeezed
freshly ground black pepper
dash of paprika or cayenne*

*1 tsp. snipped fresh parsley
small clumps green
  and purple grapes **

Line broiler tray with aluminum foil. Place breasts in tray. Squeeze lemon over chicken; sprinkle liberally with pepper, paprika or cayenne. Let chicken sit at room temperature 15 minutes. Broil quickly, turn once to brown on both sides. Garnish with parsley and grapes. Serves 3 or 4.

AFTERTHOUGHTS: This is a dieter's delight. Change flavor by using orange, grapefruit, or lime juice. Chicken is good hot or cold. Terrific for midnight suppers or Sunday picnics in the parlor. Recipe works equally well substituting thinly sliced veal scallops.

CARROT LEMON PILAF

*1 cup sliced celery
1 cup chopped green
  onions with tops
½ cup shredded carrot
2 tbsps. butter
3 cups cooked rice (cooked
  in chicken broth)*

*1 tbsp. finely grated lemon
rind
1 tsp. sea salt
¼ tsp. freshly ground black
pepper*

Sauté celery, onions, and carrot in butter until tender. Add rice, lemon rind, salt, pepper; toss lightly. Continue cooking over low heat 5 minutes or until thoroughly heated. Serve at once. Serves 6.

NOTE: Rice is a slenderizing way to include starch in the diet. For unusual touches, serve pilaf with turkey, veal, baked or broiled fish and your choice of condiments, such as raisins, sliced, chopped ripe plums, slivered butter-browned almonds, bacon crumbles, or chutney.

MINTED * PEAS

1 pkg. frozen peas
2 tbsps. butter
  *pinch of dried mint * or*
  crushed fennel

¼ tsp. sea salt
white pepper to taste
thin slice of
  white onion

Put peas in melted butter in heavy saucepan. Add mint * or fennel, salt, white pepper, and onion. Cover, heat until peas begin to simmer. Break up peas with fork; cover again. Cook over low heat until peas are barely cooked. Serve at once. Serves 4.

NOTE: Fun to do with garden-fresh peas or petits pois.

PEACH * OF A PIE

2 pie crusts, homemade or
  prepared according to
  package instructions
4 cups peeled, sliced
  peaches *
scant cup sugar (half
  brown, half white) or ¾
  cup honey
grated rind of 1 lemon
dash of sea salt

2 tsps. fresh lemon juice
¼ cup unbleached flour
½ tsp. ground mace
2 tbsps. butter or
  margarine

Line 9-inch pie dish with crust. Combine peaches, sugar or honey, lemon rind, salt, lemon juice, flour, and mace. Toss to blend ingredients. Pile lightly into pastry shell. Dot with butter or margarine. Top with upper crust. Crimp edges together to seal crusts. Cut vent holes in upper crust to allow steam to escape. Bake in preheated 425° F. 45 minutes or until crust is browned and juice begins to bubble through the slits. Serve warm or with a scoop of vanilla ice cream. Serves 6.

NOTE: Peach, the golden Venusian fruit, is delightful baked in individual tarts. Select only ripe, well-flavored fruit.

SECOND DECAN: OCTOBER 3 to OCTOBER 12

Add the qualities of Uranus: you are romantic, inventive, and independent in the kitchen.

Create the perfect opportunity to harness your most positive trait and put on a beautiful bash. It's sure to be a happening! You can create the mood with soft candlelight and romantic music or soft ballads.

Once you make up your mind about the menu, you can create a Libran dinner you enjoy as much as your guests. The pace will be leisurely and relaxed.

———

BAKED CHICKEN PARMESAN *

Vegetables Française *

Vegetable Crudité *

Bartlett Pears with Red Cherry Sauce *

Minted * Tea *

- or -

For a ladies' luncheon:

ICEBERG PUFF *

Asparagus Bundles

Honeyed Green Grapes *

Coffee or Tea

BAKED CHICKEN PARMESAN

1 3-lb. broiler-fryer chicken
cut in serving pieces
⅓ cup olive oil
2 tbsps. fresh lemon juice
¼ cup dry white wine
2 tbsps. grated Romano
cheese
2 tbsps. Parmesan cheese

¼ tsp. crushed
oregano
¼ tsp. crushed basil
1 small bay leaf,
crumbled
⅛ tsp. garlic powder
½ tsp. sea salt
few gratings freshly
ground black pepper

Place chicken skin side up in foil-lined baking dish. Pour olive oil over chicken. Combine remaining ingredients, mix well. Pour over chicken. Bake in preheated 350° F. oven 1 hour or until tender. Baste often with pan drippings. Just before serving, run under broiler to brown chicken. Spoon pan drippings over chicken. Serves 4.

VEGETABLES FRANÇAISE

1 medium head western
iceberg lettuce
2 cups water
1 tsp. sea salt
1 lb. small white boiling
onions

1 pkg. (10 oz.) frozen
green peas
⅓ cup melted butter
⅛ tsp. nutmeg
¾ tsp. tarragon

Core, rinse, thoroughly drain lettuce; chill in disposable plastic bag. Heat water with salt to boiling in covered saucepan. Add onions, cook uncovered 5 minutes. Meanwhile, place steamer basket in saucepan. Place peas in basket; sprinkle with salt. Cover, steam about 8 minutes. Shred lettuce coarsely; add to steamer basket. Steam no more than 1 minute. Mound lettuce in center of serving dish. Arrange peas and onions around lettuce. Mix butter, nutmeg and tarragon. Pour over vegetables. Serve at once. Serves 6.

VEGETABLE CRUDITÉ

parsnips
cauliflowerets
cherry tomatoes
radishes
carrot curls
green pepper rings

ripe black olives
cleaned raw mushrooms
(add few drops lemon
juice)
celery sticks

Prepare vegetables; chill well. Arrange attractively on large glass platter or individual salad plates. Serve without any adornment. Great for dieters. A great way to break the ice! This is truly a "vocal" dish.

BARTLETT PEARS WITH RED CHERRY SAUCE

6 fresh California
Bartlett pears *
boiling salted water
fresh lemon or lime juice
1½ cups Bing cherries * or
canned, drained
sweet cherries
½ cup honey

3 tbsps. unbleached flour
¼ tsp. sea salt
1 cup orange juice
1 cup rosé wine
1 tsp. aromatic bitters,
optional
¼ cup Cherry Heering
8 drops red food color

Cook pears in boiling salted water to cover about 8 minutes or until fork-tender. When cool enough to handle, remove stems, peel off skin, and cut out cores from bottom. Coat fruit with lemon or lime juice; cover tightly with Saran Wrap and chill if desired. Stem, pit cherries. Blend honey, flour, and salt in saucepan; stir in orange juice, wine, and bitters. Bring mixture to boil over medium heat, stirring constantly. Stir in Cherry Heering, food color, and cherries. Serve hot or cold. Serve each pear in a dessert dish; spoon sauce over pear. Serves 6.

NOTE: A showy, beautiful dessert! Lovely for a buffet table, too.

MINTED TEA

1½ tsps. mint flakes * or
   mint leaves *
6 tbsps. loose tea

6 tsps. honey
6 cups boiling water

Preheat teapot by rinsing out with hot water. Place tea and mint in teapot. Add honey. Fill with boiling water. Let stand 5 minutes; stir. Strain before serving. Serves 6.

NOTE: Serve cold in tall glasses; garnish with lemon or lime slices.

ICEBERG PUFF

2 heads western
   iceberg lettuce
½ cup salted water
3 tbsps. butter
2 tbsps. cornstarch
½ tsp. sea salt

¼ tsp. marjoram
⅛ tsp. white pepper
¾ cup half-and-half or
   light cream
4 eggs, separated

Core, rinse and drain lettuce; store in refrigerator in plastic crisper or disposable plastic bag. Coarsely chop enough lettuce to measure 8 cups, lightly packed. Place lettuce in large kettle with salted water. Stirring often, cook, covered, 5 minutes or until barely crisp. Drain. Melt butter in saucepan; blend in cornstarch, salt, marjoram, and pepper. Stir in half-and-half and cook, stirring, until mixture comes to a boil and thickens. Fold prepared lettuce and egg yolks into white sauce. Whip whites until stiff peaks form, and fold into yolk mixture. Turn into greased 2-quart soufflé dish or casserole. Place dish in pan of hot water. Bake in preheated 350° F. oven 1 hour. Serve at once. Serves 6.

NOTE: A perfect make-ahead main dish for the Libran lady who likes light airy fare. Lettuce in puff eliminates need for salad and will be a conversation piece with your guests.

HONEYED GREEN GRAPES

1 lb. Thompson seedless
  *grapes **
1 tsp. fresh lemon or lime
  juice
¼ cup honey

2 tbsps. sherry or brandy
½ cup dairy sour cream
8 to 12 large
  *strawberries, * washed*
  lemon leaves, optional

Wash, stem grapes. Mix lemon juice, honey, and sherry or brandy; pour over grapes. Pour into silver serving dish. Freeze until firm. Allow 15 minutes before serving. Scoop out on glass dishes. Garnish each plate with strawberries and lemon leaves. Serves 4 to 6.

NOTE: A lovely Venusian dessert.

THIRD DECAN: OCTOBER 13 to OCTOBER 22

Add the qualities of Mars and you become more dynamic, ambitious, yet restless and impulsive. Your seasonings even take on Martian-like qualities. Your usual subtle fare becomes spicier or hotter. Follow your natural instinct for balance; don't overseason the food. Create supper menus to turn on the romance in your life!

———

BEEF CONSOMMÉ GARNISHED WITH CHIVES *

Onion * Soufflé *

Buttered Carrots Seasoned with Rosemary

Garlic * Bread

Super Cranberry Apple Pie *

- or -

BEST BEEF CHILI YET *

Hot Cooked Brown Rice

Romaine Lettuce Salad

Spicy Oranges *

ONION * SOUFFLÉ

1 lb. onions, peeled
4 tbsps. butter
4 tbsps. unbleached flour
⅓ cup water in which
    onions were cooked

⅓ cup half-and-half
sea salt, white pepper
    to taste
3 egg yolks, slightly beaten
4 egg whites, beaten
    until stiff

Boil onions until soft. Drain, chop. Melt butter, add flour; gradually add onion water and half-and-half, stirring. Season to taste. Add onion pulp and bring to boiling point. Add to beaten egg yolks. Fold in egg whites. Turn into buttered (on bottom only) baking dish. Place in pan of hot water. Bake in preheated 375° F. oven 40 minutes. Serve at once! Serves 6.

NOTE: A luscious soufflé for onion-lovers. Inexpensive, too!

SUPER CRANBERRY APPLE PIE

1 pie crust (homemade or
prepared)
1 can (1 lb.) whole berry
cranberry sauce
2 tbsps. quick-cooking
tapioca

4 to 5 tart apples, * *pared,*
cored, thinly sliced
1½ cups fresh cranberries
1 cup pineapple preserves

Roll out pastry in round large enough to line bottom and side of a 12-inch pizza pan. Flute a high edge. Mix together cranberry sauce and tapioca; spread mixture evenly over crust. Top with ring of apple slices around the edge of the crust. Place remaining apple slices in center to form circle. Mix together cranberries and preserves in saucepan. Simmer, stirring constantly, until cranberries are tender, about 5 minutes. Spoon mixture over apple slices. Bake in preheated 425° F. oven 20 minutes or until crust is brown and fruit is tender. Cool to lukewarm before slicing. Or serve cold with ice cream or whipped cream. Makes one 12-inch pie.

NOTE: A terrific way to combine tart red cranberries and apples to celebrate fall!

BEST BEEF CHILI YET

3½ lbs. lean beef chuck or
  bottom round
5 tbsps. vegetable oil
2 onions, peeled, chopped
4 cloves garlic,* minced
3 tbsps. chili powder
1½ tsps. oregano
1 tsp. cumin
½ tsp. cayenne *

1 can (10½ oz.) condensed
  beef broth
1 can (28 oz.) tomatoes
1 can (6 oz.) tomato paste
1 tbsp. sea salt
1 tsp. honey, optional
1 to 2 tbsps. cornmeal
hot cooked rice

Cut beef into ½-inch cubes. Heat 3 tbsps. oil in large heavy pot. Add beef all at once. Sear it, turning constantly, until lightly browned. Remove beef; set it aside. Add remaining 2 tbsps. oil, onion, and garlic.* Sauté until onion is limp. Stir in chili powder, oregano, cumin, and cayenne,* coating onion. Return beef to pot. Add water to broth to measure 2 cups liquid. Add to beef along with tomatoes, tomato paste, salt, and honey, mixing well. Cover, simmer 1 hour. Uncover and simmer 45 minutes until beef is very tender. Cool. Cover, refrigerate overnight. Heat to serve. Thicken with cornmeal as needed. Serve with rice. Serves 8 generously.

SPICY ORANGES

2 cans (10½ oz. each)
  mandarin oranges
½ cup dry red wine
¼ cup honey
¼ tsp. finely grated lime or
  lemon peel

¼ tsp. finely grated orange
  peel
4 whole cloves
1 3-inch stick cinnamon

Drain oranges; set aside. Combine wine, honey, lime and orange peel, cloves, and cinnamon in small saucepan. Bring to boil; simmer 5 minutes. Pour mixture over oranges. Cover, chill several hours or overnight. Remove spices before serving. Place oranges in tall crystal sherbet glasses. Spoon some of the wine sauce over each portion. Serves 4.

SCORPIO: OCTOBER 23 to NOVEMBER 21

Mystery Food!

SINCE YOU ARE ruled by both Mars and Pluto, you are seldom ignored because people either adore you or hate you!

Outwardly, you display unusual self-control, even though inwardly you may be banking red-hot coals. You have intense feeling about anything you undertake in life, including foods in general and cooking. Your eating habits are a dead giveaway to your sign. While you possess a most unorthodox palate, craving hot dogs, you also revel in such succulent delights as mandarin duck or nice thick juicy steaks. You have insisted upon certain foods ever since you bypassed your pablum for the onion rings with the hamburger and the crisp skin on the roasted chicken!

You are never puny-looking since you crave good living and good eating. Typically, you like food that smacks of mystery and originality. While other people want to know exactly what they are eating, you prefer novel fare that is exotic, highly spiced, often hot or elaborate.

You love to entertain or be entertained on Tuesdays by other water types: Cancerians or Pisceans.

FIRST DECAN: OCTOBER 23 to NOVEMBER 2

Bone-building foods, such as milk, cheese, eggs, seafood, watercress, kale, cabbage, and prunes, those containing phosphorus, potassium, and calcium, are important to you. Because you are literally hung up on eating terrific Italian pasta, eat other starches and sugar sparingly. Your food tastes are similar to Arieans, with special emphasis on well-seasoned delights like chili, Italian, Spanish, and Mexican dishes.

Watch eating or drinking to excess; be frugal with the pepper,* mustard,* hops, and alcoholic beverages! Since it's vital to you to seek the ultimate expression of your body, mind, and will, remember: Food and drink must minister to the spirit if it is not to go into the stomach like sand and water into a well-oiled machine. Remember, Scorpio, you eat to live; not the other way around!

SCORPIONIAN BRUNCH-LUNCH

Prune Juice

Eggs Scorpio *   Bacon Chive * Corn Muffins *

Hot Chocolate

- or -

VEAL PARMESAN OR CORNISH HENS ROYALE

Nutty Zucchini Stir *

Eighth House Egg-Onion * Salad Mold *

Baked Apple Crisp

Milk

EGGS SCORPIO

3 tbsps. onion,* chopped
¼ cup celery, sliced
¼ cup green pepper,*
  chopped
2 tbsps. vegetable oil
3 tbsps. unbleached flour
1 can (6 oz.) mushrooms,
  drained, sliced

1 can (16 oz.) tomatoes
1 tsp. sea salt
¾ tsp. chili powder
6 hard-cooked eggs,
  coarsely chopped
6 English muffins, split,
  toasted
chopped fresh parsley *

Cook raw vegetables in oil until tender. Blend in flour. Stir in mushrooms, tomatoes, salt, and chili powder; blend well. Gently mix in eggs. Heat thoroughly over medium heat, stirring occasionally to scramble. Serve on toasted English muffins. Garnish with parsley. Serves 6.

BACON CHIVE * CORN MUFFINS

1 (12 oz.) pkg. corn muffin
  mix
2 tsps. chopped chives *
dash freshly ground black
  pepper

1 egg
⅔ cup milk
½ cup crisp bacon crumbles

In large bowl combine corn muffin mix, chives,* and pepper. Add egg and milk according to package directions. Fold in crumbled bacon. Turn into 12 greased 2¾-inch muffin tins. Bake in preheated 400° F. oven 20 to 25 minutes or until done. Serve hot with plenty of butter. Makes 12 muffins.

NUTTY ZUCCHINI STIR

½ lb. zucchini
½ cup sliced onion *
¼ cup vegetable oil
¼ cup dry red wine
2 tbsps. lemon juice

⅛ tsp. grated lemon rind
½ cup water
1 cup coarsely chopped nuts

Cut zucchini in 1-inch slices. Sauté zucchini and onions in oil 5 minutes, stirring frequently. Add wine, lemon juice and rind, and water. Simmer 5 minutes. Add nuts. Serves 6.

NOTE: A boon to the Scorpionian gardener who gets carried away and harvests a carload of zucchini! Dish gets its name because it literally causes a stir when served! Great, too, for vegetarians! Zucchini is a fine vegetable, low in calories—about 19 calories per ½ cup cooked serving—with small amounts of vitamins and minerals.

EIGHTH HOUSE EGG-ONION * SALAD MOLD

1 tbsp. unflavored gelatin
¼ cup cold water
½ cup boiling water
6 eggs, hard-cooked,
  chopped
¼ cup scallions,*
  chopped
½ cup radishes,*
  chopped
1 tsp. prepared mustard

½ tsp. Worcestershire
  sauce
½ tsp. sea salt
⅛ tsp. freshly ground
  pepper
½ cup bottled French
  dressing
crisp salad greens:
  lettuce, chicory

Soften gelatin in cold water. Dissolve softened gelatin in boiling water. Add remaining ingredients except salad greens; mix well. Pour into a 1-quart mold or 6 individual molds. Chill mixture in mold in refrigerator until it sets. Unmold on a bed of crisp salad greens. Serves 6.

SECOND DECAN: NOVEMBER 3 to NOVEMBER 12

Add the qualities of Neptune, and you add the foresight, adaptability, and spiritual qualities that fit your personality. You may confuse your friends, however, because you sometimes seem vague, with a tendency to deceive simply because you don't like to expose your deepest thoughts.

There's no confusion about your food passions, Scorpio! Make it either Chinese or Italian and you're in heaven! You may even take it to your work if you're a man, but you're more likely to bring home the recipe to get your mother or girl friend to prepare that production for you. Since you are very persuasive and charming, it's not hard to realize your most outlandish Scorpionian desires!

CHICKEN SUBGUM SCORPIO * or DUCK A LA SCORPIO *

Hot Steamed Rice   Duck Sauce (good bottled variety)

Green Tea   Fresh Pineapple (or water-pack)

Fortune Cookies

- or -

HERBED EGGPLANT CASSEROLE *

Iceberg Lettuce Wedges   Roquefort Dressing

Fruit Bowl: Yellow Apples, Grapes, Banana, and Oranges

- or -

BEEF DOLMADES WITH TOMATO SAUCE *

Sliced Tomatoes   Hot Bran Rolls *

CHICKEN SUBGUM SCORPIO

2 cups raw chicken or
turkey, cut in small dice
3 tbsps. cooking oil
½ cup onion,* diced
1 can (4 oz.) chop suey
vegetables
½ can (4 oz.) water
chestnuts, diced
½ can (4 oz.) bamboo
shoots, diced

1 cup button mushrooms
2 cups chicken stock
2 tbsps. soy sauce
½ cup white wine
(or grapefruit juice)
2 tsps. cornstarch
½ cup pine nuts,*
chopped
almonds
½ green pepper, sliced

Fry chicken or turkey in hot oil until lightly browned. Add all
other ingredients except cornstarch, pine nuts,* and garnish.
Cover, cook for about 10 minutes. Mix cornstarch with a little
water, add to chicken mixture. Cook until sauce is slightly
thickened, stirring. Remove from fire; stir in almonds. Decorate
with almonds and green peppers. Serve with steamed rice or
chow mein noodles. Serves 4.

DUCK A LA SCORPIO

For the orange sauce:

1 (11 oz.) can mandarin
   oranges
¼ cup frozen orange juice,
   undiluted
1 clove garlic, pressed

¼ tsp. dry mustard*
½ tsp. sea salt
1 tbsp. cornstarch
¼ cup water

Mix together first 5 ingredients in saucepan. Bring to boil. Let cook 10 minutes. Mix cornstarch with water; pour into pan. Stir until mixture thickens. Set aside.

For the duck:

1 cleaned, dressed duck,
   weighing 4 or 5 lbs.
1 tsp. sea salt

¼ freshly ground
   black pepper
1 tbsp. sake

Wash, dry duck. Rub outside and inside cavity with salt and pepper. Sprinkle sake into cavity. Place duck on rack in roasting pan. Roast in preheated 425° F. oven 30 minutes. Reduce oven temperature to 375°F. Continue roasting 1½ hours longer, pouring out melted fat frequently. Serve on platter with heated orange sauce poured over duck. Serves 4.

HERBED EGGPLANT CASSEROLE

3 tbsps. sweet pepper *
  flakes
2 tbsps. celery flakes
1½ tbsps. instant
  minced onion*
⅛ tsp. instant minced
  garlic *
⅓ cup water
6 slices bacon
⅓ cup pine nuts *
1 lb. lean ground beef
1 can (16 oz.) tomatoes

1 can (6 oz.) tomato paste
½ tsp. basil leaves
½ tsp. sea salt
¼ tsp. cayenne
¼ tsp. freshly ground
  black pepper
1 bay leaf
2 medium-size eggplants,
  1 lb. each
boiling water
1 tsp. salt
1½ cups grated Cheddar
  or Mozzarella cheese

Combine first five ingredients; let stand 5 minutes to soften vegetables. Meanwhile, in large skillet, fry bacon until partially cooked. Remove to absorbent paper. Add softened vegetables and pine nuts * to bacon fat. Cook over low heat, stirring frequently, until onion * is lightly browned. Add beef, cook, stirring often, until brown. In large mixing bowl, combine tomatoes, tomato paste, basil, salt, cayenne, black pepper, and bay leaf. Add to beef mixture. Cook, uncovered, over low heat, stirring frequently until thickened, about 40 minutes. Meanwhile, slice unpeeled eggplants crosswise in ½-inch slices. Place in large amount of boiling salted water. Cook 5 minutes. Drain eggplant on absorbent paper. In buttered 2-quart casserole place layer of eggplant; top with tomato sauce and cheese. Repeat until all ingredients have been used. Cover, bake in preheated 350° F. oven 30 minutes. Remove cover. Top with reserved bacon. Bake 10 minutes longer to crispen bacon. Serves 6.

NOTE: A fabulous meal-in-one for Scorpios who dote on delicious Italian-inspired fare, made hot by the addition of the "hot" foods of Mars: garlic, onion and pepper. Pine nuts, a favorite food of Neptune, are often found in Italian dishes (available in supermarkets).

BEEF DOLMADES WITH TOMATO SAUCE

8 *large cabbage leaves*
2 *lbs. ground beef*
½ *cup uncooked rice*
2 *eggs, beaten*
1 *large onion, * finely chopped*

1–2 *drops pressed garlic * juice*
2 *tsps. sea salt*
½ *tsp. freshly ground black pepper*
¼ *tsp. rosemary*
½ *tsp. celery salt*

Core large head of cabbage; remove 8 leaves. Trim off thick part of leaves and cover with boiling water; let stand 5 minutes. Meanwhile, mix together beef, eggs, rice, onion, and seasonings. Remove leaves from water; drain. Place equal portions of mixture on each of the 8 leaves and roll up. Fasten each cabbage bundle with toothpicks to keep filling in. Place each dolmade seam side down in heavy skillet or casserole. Pour tomato sauce over; cover and bake in preheated 350° F. oven 1 hour. Remove cover and bake ½ hour longer. Baste as necessary with the sauce during cooking.

TOMATO SAUCE

3 *cans (8 oz. each) tomato sauce*
1 *cup beef bouillon or broth*
1 *small green pepper, finely chopped*

2 *tbsps. honey*
¼ *tsp. rosemary*
1 *large onion, * peeled, finely chopped*
1 *tbsp. chopped parsley **
1 *tsp. sea salt*
½ *tsp. cracked pepper*

Mix thoroughly; pour over dolmades.

HOT BRAN ROLLS

6 tbsps. butter or
    margarine
2 cups all-purpose flour
½ tsp. sea salt
1 tbsp. baking powder
¼ tsp. ground mace

¼ cup granulated sugar
¾ cup 100% bran
1 egg, well beaten
⅓ cup milk
⅔ cup apricot preserves
¼ cup water

Melt 1 tbsp. butter; set aside. Sift together flour, salt, baking powder, and mace. Cut in 4 tbsps. butter until texture is like coarse cornmeal. Stir in sugar and bran. Make a well in center; add combined egg and milk. Mix until blended; then knead until smooth on a lightly floured board. Divide in half. Roll one half into a circle, about 10 inches in diameter. Brush with half of melted butter. Cut into 8 triangles. Place about ½ tsp. preserves on broad end of triangles. Repeat with remainder of dough. Bake in preheated 400° F. oven 10 to 15 minutes, or until done. Makes about 16 rolls. Meanwhile, combine remainder of preserves with water. Stir and bring to a boil. Boil 3 minutes without stirring. Remove from heat; stir in remaining butter. Remove rolls to rack. Brush with glaze. Serve warm.

NOTE: Terrific tasting. Unusual made with blueberry preserves.

THIRD DECAN: NOVEMBER 13 to NOVEMBER 21

Add the influence of Jupiter and you are your most gracious self! Your optimism, expansiveness, and general benevolence toward everyone make you a super host or hostess. Predictably, you seek out the "ultra" in restaurants. You feel you squandered or gladly spent your loot according to the quality of the meal.

Sagittarians will gladly share your family board although they are not as hung up on food as you are. Your table talk with a "Sag" should be stimulating and enlightening. The meal should match the mood. Now is the time to head for a terrific Mexican place. If that's not possible, or you'd rather relax at home, create a Scorpio sensation with a Tostadas Fiesta party!

CONSOMMÉ OR MARGARITA

Tostadas Fiesta! *

Lemon Meringue Pie or Fresh Fruit Bowl

Beer or Coffee

TOSTADAS FIESTA!

For the guacamole:

2 *soft California avocados,*
peeled, coarsely mashed
¾ *tsp. seasoned salt*
1 *tbsp. fresh lemon*
or lime juice

¼ *tsp. Worcestershire*
sauce
2 *tbsps. freshly grated*
onion

Mix ingredients with fork. Cover tightly; store in refrigerator until ready to use.

For spiced meat mixture:

1 *pkg. taco seasoning mix*

1 *lb. lean boneless*
ground round

Brown beef, stirring until crumbly. Drain off fat; discard. Add seasoning to beef with water according to taco mix instructions. Simmer as directed. Makes enough filling for 8 tostados.

For the tortillas:

8 *corn tortillas, preferably*
fresh if available (or use
canned or frozen)

oil for frying

Fry tortillas in hot oil until crisp. Drain on paper towels. This can be done 1 hour in advance of serving time. Keep warm in 200° F. oven or make them several hours ahead. Let them stand at room temperature. Rewarm them 30 minutes before serving in 200° F. oven.

Directions to assemble
tostadas:

8 prepared warm tortillas   *warm spiced meat*
heated, refried beans   *mixture*
(20 oz. can)   *1 small head of lettuce,*
1 cup shredded Jack cheese   *shredded*
1 cup shredded Cheddar   *2 peeled, sliced tomatoes*
cheese

Keep tortillas flat. Top each warm tortilla with layer of refried beans, grated cheeses, warm spiced beef, lettuce, and tomatoes. Top with guacamole. Terrific eating for 4 hungry people!

NOTE: Since tostadas are a glorious combination of salad, meat, vegetable, and bread, 2 tostadas are very filling. Variations on the classic tostadas are infinite!

Substitute for spiced meat mixture:
2 cups cold, sliced chicken, turkey, pork, shrimp, or crab

Substitute for guacamole:
sour cream (1 pint), sliced, ripe avocado (one medium) plus
taco sauce

Substitute for refried beans:
canned kidney beans doctored to suit your palate. Or use
*leftover baked beans spiked with garlic * and/or onion **

Garnishes: pickled red, green, hot, or mild chilies

Fortunately, all the ingredients for the Scorpionians' Fiesta delight are available in most supermarkets!

TACO SAUCE

2 medium canned
  tomatoes, drained,
  mashed with fork
¼ cup diced green chili
1 small onion,* peeled,
  coarsely chopped

2 tbsps. diced green
  pepper *
1 cup vinegar
1 tsp. sea salt
¼ tsp. garlic * powder
⅛ tsp. oregano
⅛ tsp. ground cumin

Mix ingredients; let it stand at room temperature 1 hour.
Refrigerate until ready to use.

SAGITTARIUS: NOVEMBER 22 to DECEMBER 21

Keep It Simple!

LIKE YOUR SIGN, the archer, you aim for the stars. Invariably, you achieve your goals because of your drive.

You are a deep thinker with an uncanny knack for knowing exactly what's going on in people's heads. Typically, you give that same concentration to selecting a menu or performing at the range.

You have a thing about travel and enjoy food from many places. Saturday is your magic day for entertaining. Your favorite guests are other fire people like yourself or Arieans and Leonians. You have a hearty appetite and prefer down-to-earth food from all over the globe served simply but elegantly. Your standards are high. You judge your own cooking ability and that of others by the way they prepare simple, one-dish meals (stews, soups, or casseroles).

You are one of the few signs under the Zodiac that enjoy English- as well as American-type fare.

Remember to provide infinite variety. Never overlook the vegetables but don't clutter up the stew with too many.

FIRST DECAN: NOVEMBER 22 to DECEMBER 1

You enjoy entertaining expansively, and you're often extravagant! You are fond of exotic dishes, but be careful not to overindulge in sugars, starches or other fattening foods.

Due to your universal outlook, you reduce your thoughts and feelings to down-to-earth fundamentals. Your food is like the arrows that feed the bow of Sagittarius: Watch your diet carefully and don't get carried away by the exotic excitement of it all. Follow in Sagittarius' footsteps with something simple, such as a delicious leg of lamb with mint sauce.

Your food favorites include chervil,* mushrooms,* peas,* asparagus,* endive,* currants,* jasmine * tea, and rose hips. *

LUSCIOUS LEG OF LAMB WITH MINT SAUCE *

Asparagus or Braised Endive *   Baked Potato

Bananas Flambé *   Jasmine * Tea

- or -

STEAK DIANE

Saged * Pears   Snow Peas With Water Chestnuts *

Health Buns *   Sweet Butter and Honey

Rose Hips Tea *

LUSCIOUS LEG OF LAMB WITH MINT SAUCE

4 tbsps. dried mint flakes
1 cup white vinegar
2 scant tbsps. honey
1 7 to 8 lb. leg of lamb
pickled crab apples or
cinnamon apple rings

cut lime or lemon
sea salt
freshly ground pepper to
taste
parsley or watercress

Combine mint flakes, vinegar, and honey. Simmer 5 minutes; set aside. Place lamb on rack in shallow roasting pan. Rub outside with lime or lemon. Sprinkle liberally with salt, pepper. Insert meat thermometer in fleshy part of leg; avoid hitting bone. Bake in preheated 300° F. oven 3½ hours (or until thermometer registers between 170° and 180° F.). Lamb lovers like theirs rare at 170° F.! Allow roast to firm up before carving. Garnish with parsley or watercress. Pass mint sauce. Serves 8.

NOTE: If desired, insert tiny bits of garlic into roast before roasting.

BRAISED ENDIVE *

*8 stalks Belgian endive **
chicken broth
1 tbsp. butter or margarine
sea salt

freshly ground pepper to
taste
dash of lemon juice

Arrange whole endives in shallow saucepan. Add a little chicken broth. Cover, braise about 7 minutes or until barely tender. Add butter or margarine. Cool few minutes longer or until most of the liquid has been absorbed. Season lightly with salt, pepper, and lemon juice. Serves 4.

BANANAS FLAMBÉ

4 bananas
3 tbsps. butter
4 tsps. confectioners' sugar

3 tbsps. 150-proof dark
   rum
vanilla ice cream or
   whipped cream, optional

Peel and slice bananas. Sauté in butter in chafing dish or skillet suitable for serving at table. When bananas are golden, dust with confectioners' sugar. Spoon 2 tbsps. rum into chafing dish or skillet; set aflame, bring flaming to table. Spoon up rum to make certain alcohol burns out completely. Add remaining rum if desired, making sure all the alcohol burns out. Serve alone or with ice cream or whipped cream. Serves 4 to 8.

NOTE: A dramatic finish to a delightful meal. Since dessert is rich, allow ½ to 1 banana per serving.

SNOW PEAS WITH WATER CHESTNUTS

1 tsp. peanut oil
½ lb. snow peas (or frozen,
   thawed), cut in half,
   lengthwise

1 small can water
   chestnuts, drained, sliced,
   slivered
2 to 3 tbsps. chicken broth
soy sauce to taste, optional

Heat oil in wok or skillet over high heat. Add remaining ingredients; stir-fry over high heat 2 or 3 minutes. Serves 4 to 6.

HEALTH BUNS

1 pkg. active dry yeast	*⅓ cup wheat germ*
2¼ cups buttermilk	*½ cup currants*
1 tsp. sea salt	*1½ cups unbleached*
1¼ cups whole rye flour	*flour*
1¼ cups whole wheat flour	

Dissolve yeast in ¼ cup lukewarm water in mixing bowl. Add next 6 ingredients; stir with wooden spoon until blended. Gradually add unbleached flour, beating until smooth. Turn out on floured board. Knead until smooth and elastic; let rise 30 minutes. Divide dough in 12 equal balls; place in well-greased muffin tins. Let rise 1 hour, or until doubled in bulk. Bake in preheated 400° F. oven 30 minutes, or until done. Cool on rack. Makes 1 dozen buns.

ROSE HIPS * TEA

*4 heaping tsps. rose hips *	*½ lemon, sliced*
4 cups boiling water	*honey, optional*

Steep rose hips in boiling water 10 minutes. Add lemon, strain and serve. Serves 4.

NOTE: In Ireland, black currant leaves and rose hips are brewed with regular tea. The mixture is lovely and aromatic. Nutritionally, rose hips are lovely, too! This "fruit of the rose" is one of the best sources of vitamin C known to man, as well as an excellent source of phosphorus, calcium, and iron.

SECOND DECAN: DECEMBER 2 to DECEMBER 11

Now add the qualities of Mercury: you are quick-witted and mentally alert. It's reflected in your cooking because you are versatile and adaptable. You tend to favor way-out dishes made with odd herbs, spices, and vegetables. Temper your impulses even though, like Martians, you like onions and horseradish in salads, chili or pepperpot.*

Be on guard that your constant desire for change and excitement doesn't make you act fickle and bored with your guests. Entertaining at one-dish lunches is the perfect answer to beat boredom!

FRESH ORANGE JUICE. WELL CHILLED

Planetary Vegetable Egg Bundles *

or Seafood Stuffed Tomatoes *

Mixed Raw Vegetable Platter

Sesame Seed Rolls   Fresh Fruit Cup

- or -

JOVIAN PEPPERPOT *

Homemade Noodles *   Carrots

Key Lime Pie *

PLANETARY VEGETABLE EGG BUNDLES

1 pkg. frozen asparagus *
spears
1 can (4 oz.) sliced
mushrooms
1 cup medium white sauce
or 1 cup canned
condensed mushroom
soup

4 English muffins, split
butter or margarine
4 poached eggs
½ cup mayonnaise or salad
dressing
2 tbsps. dairy sour cream
2 tbsps. fresh lemon juice

Cook asparagus * according to package instructions; drain well. Drain mushrooms; add to white sauce (or mushroom soup). Heat in saucepan over low heat. Toast muffins and butter each half lightly; arrange on serving plate. Divide asparagus spears between 4 muffin halves; cover with mushroom soup or white sauce. Place poached eggs on remaining 4 muffins. Combine ingredients for lemon sauce by blending together mayonnaise, sour cream, and lemon juice, and pour sauce over egg bundles. Serves 4.

SEAFOOD STUFFED TOMATOES

*1 pkg. (7 oz.) frozen
shrimp or 1 cup cooked
shrimp
1 pkg. (6 oz.) frozen crab
meat, thawed and well
drained
1 cup grated carrot *
1 chopped hard-cooked egg
2 tbsps. sliced green onion
1 cup dairy sour cream
2 tbsps. chopped
fresh parsley **

*2 tbsps. grated lime *
or lemon rind
2 tbsps. fresh lime * or
lemon juice
1 tsp. prepared
yellow mustard
1 tsp. sea salt
freshly ground
black pepper to taste
6 large ripe tomatoes*

Cut shrimp into small pieces; flake crab meat. Combine
shrimp, crab meat, carrot, egg, and onion; chill. Meanwhile,
combine sour cream, parsley, lime (or lemon rind), and juice,
mustard, salt, and pepper. Chill. Remove slice from stem and
blossom ends of tomatoes. Place each tomato on its side; cut
into thirds about ⅔ way down. Stuff about ½ cup seafood
mixture between sections of each tomato. Serves 6.

JOVIAN PEPPERPOT

For the noodles:

2 eggs
½ tsp. salt

1½ cups unbleached flour

Beat eggs with salt until blended. Stir in enough flour to make soft paste. Knead dough on heavily floured board until smooth and elastic. Roll out to paper thinness; cut into 1½-inch squares with sharp knife. Let noodles dry on cloth several hours while preparing meat.

For soup-stew:

1½ lbs. beef chuck, cubed
1 green pepper, chopped
1 onion, peeled and chopped

2 potatoes, peeled and diced
1 tbsp. Angostura aromatic bitters
2 cans (10½ oz. each) condensed beef broth

Cover beef with water; simmer covered until meat is tender (about 2 hours). Add remaining ingredients to meat with noodles. Add 2 more cups of water. Cover, simmer 15 minutes (or until noodles and potatoes are tender). Season to taste with salt and pepper. Serves 4.

KEY LIME PIE

8-inch baked pie shell or
prepared crushed vanilla
wafer crust
4 eggs, separated
1 can (15 oz.) sweetened
condensed milk
2 tbsps. butter, melted

1 tbsp. finely grated lime *
rind
⅓ cup fresh lime * juice
dash sea salt
½ cup honey
¼ tsp. pure vanilla extract

Prepare crust as directed. Beat egg yolks lightly; blend with milk, butter, lime rind, and juice. Pour into pie shell. Beat egg whites and salt until frothy. Gradually add honey, beat until stiff and glossy. Fold in vanilla. Pile meringue on top of filling. Bake in preheated 325° F. oven 20 minutes or until meringue is golden. Chill well before serving. Serves 6.

THIRD DECAN: DECEMBER 12 to DECEMBER 21

Add the qualities of Saturn and you appear more down to earth. You are ambitious, thrifty, persevering, but sometimes slow and impatient. If you don't achieve your goals, you are gloomy!

Try and plan menus within your energy and budget limits. Since the holidays may be almost upon you, one-dish meals are a terrific way to entertain in style. Combine potatoes, barley * in stews to satisfy your Saturnian influences. Step up milk and cheese consumption to keep healthy and strong for the new year ahead.

SAGITTARIAN VEGETABLE DINNER DIVINE *

- or -

SIMPLY HEAVENLY PORK IN A STEW *

or Bagged Mexican Roast with Vegetables *

Pickled Beet * Relish-Egg Salad *

Saffron * Cookies   Skimmed Milk

SAGITTARIAN VEGETABLE DINNER DIVINE

1 cup brown rice
2 cups green lima beans
(frozen, preferably)
1 cup (3 oz. can or frozen)
green peas *
1 cup sliced carrots
½ cup sliced fresh
mushrooms *
1 tsp. ground sage *

½ tsp. chervil *
2 chicken bouillon cubes
½ cup cauliflowerets
1 cup fresh broccoli
pieces
1 California avocado
1 tbsp. chopped fresh
parsley

Combine all ingredients except cauliflower, broccoli, avocado, and parsley in 2-quart saucepan. Bring to boil. Cook 35 minutes. Add cauliflower and broccoli. Cook additional 10 minutes. Spoon into heat-proof 2-quart casserole dish. Halve, peel and slice avocado. Garnish with parsley. Serves 6.

NOTE: This Jovian treat features a trio of astrological favorites: peas, mushrooms, and chervil. Nonvegetarians like the stew made with strips of cooked boneless veal or chicken. Aztec Indians, who were sun worshipers, considered avocados an important part of their diet. Avocados are rich in vitamin A, several B vitamins, C and E, and contain a good amount of iron.

SIMPLY HEAVENLY PORK IN A STEW

2½ lbs. pork chops
3 stalks celery with leaves
4 small onions
4 potatoes, peeled, cut in large pieces
3 carrots, peeled, cut in pieces
1 clove garlic, pressed
2 sprigs fresh parsley
½ tsp. dill seed or ground sage
large pinch dried thyme

1 bay leaf
1½ tsps. salt
freshly ground black pepper to taste
about 2½ cups dry red wine or cranberry juice
1 lb. cleaned spinach or one pkg. (10 oz.) frozen leaf spinach

Trim excess fat from pork. Broil on both sides. Cool. Drain off fat from broiler pan; reserve pan drippings to flavor stew. Put celery, onions, potatoes, carrots, garlic, parsley, dill or sage, thyme, bay leaf, salt, and pepper in large saucepan. Add about 2 cups wine or cranberry juice. Bring to boil; simmer uncovered about 20 minutes. Dice pork, add to saucepan with pork bones and pan drippings. Add more wine or cranberry juice as needed. Cover, simmer 35 minutes longer. Uncover, add spinach, cook until barely tender and most of the liquid has been absorbed. Serves 4 to 6.

AFTERTHOUGHTS: As its name implies, my stew is delightful and colorful; great to serve on a chilly winter day. Include other vegetables: tomatoes, corn, broccoli, zucchini, squash, green peas, Brussels sprouts, watercress, and water chestnuts. If desired, substitute barley for potatoes.

BAGGED MEXICAN ROAST WITH VEGETABLES

1 4-lb. beef chuck roast   *8 small whole onions,*
(arm or blade cut)   *peeled*
unbleached flour   *1 bay leaf*
sea salt   *⅓ cup water*
freshly ground black   *1 ripe tomato, sliced*
pepper   *guacamole sauce*
                                    hot baby carrots for garnish

Trim fat from roast; rub both sides with flour. Sprinkle salt and
pepper on both sides of roast. Put meat in see-through bag for
oven (size for meats up to 6 lbs.). Place meat and bag in
roasting pan; add onions, bay leaf, and water. Close bag by
placing twist tie about 2 inches from roast; cut off excess bag.
Puncture six to eight evenly spaced holes in top of bag with
paring knife. Cook in preheated 300°F. oven 4 hours (or until
tender). Just before serving, place roast on heated platter. Skim
fat from roast juices; use juices as gravy to serve with roast.
Place overlapping row of tomato slices diagonally across top of
roast; spoon over half of guacamole. Garnish with cooked
onions and carrots. Pass rest of guacamole sauce in small
serving dish. Serves 8.

PICKLED BEET * RELISH-EGG SALAD

*1 jar (1 lb.) pickled beets ***   *bottled diet French*
6 hard-cooked eggs   *dressing or plain yogurt,*
lettuce leaves   *optional*

Drain beets; reserve juice. Place hard-cooked eggs in beet juice.
Cover, refrigerate several hours or overnight, turning occasionally to pickle evenly. To serve, drain off juice. Cut eggs in
lengthwise slices. Arrange egg, sliced beets * on lettuce leaves.
Drizzle with French dressing or yogurt. Serves 6.

CAPRICORN: DECEMBER 22 to JANUARY 19

Cook in Advance!

Since you're ruled by Saturn, the guru planet, you are pragmatic and approach life with determination, ambition, and great organization. Even during the busiest holidays of the year, you seem able to hold up under tremendous pressure, keeping your cool, planning marvelous food treats to celebrate the occasion.

You almost seem to have a blueprint for life. That extends to your kitchen as well. Typically you like to plan menus a week in advance, make yard-long lists for marketing and tuck cooking chores in between a busy career and your family.

Your family always comes first. You like to cook in advance, planning meals down to the last detail—so ambitiously it looks like you had all kinds of kitchen help. Capricorns work best alone. Your astrological food list is short (barley,* beets,* saffron,* and quince *), but you're long on ideas. Guard your energies. Load up on a diet rich in calcium. Since you value harmony above all else in life, choose dinner guests carefully. You're happiest entertaining on Saturday in the company of other earthlings like Taureans and Virgonians!

FIRST DECAN: DECEMBER 22 to DECEMBER 31

You're an early riser, hard worker, and thrive on cooking in three-quarter time! You're apt to cook enough vegetable soup to serve today and freeze the remainder to have during the busy holiday ahead.

You're happiest fixing holiday treats for your family and friends to share. You're determined to have the "good life," especially at home. Therefore, you cook up a whole carload of great food to freeze so that later you can proudly bring on all those wonderful holiday treasures.

CHRISTMAS DINNER

Turkey Pâté * with Melba Rounds

Roast Turkey Extraordinaire *   Jeane's Turkey Stock *

Williamsburg Inn Oysters *

Cranberry Apple Relish *

Sweet Potato Puffs in Orange Shells *

Broccoli

Blueberry Compote *   Various Christmas Cookies *

Hot Lemon Tea   Coffee

- or -

JEANE'S SOUP *

Carrot Curls and Celery   Saltines

Noodle Kugel with Cherry Sauce *

Hot Tea

TURKEY PÂTÉ

cooked, cooled turkey liver	*¾ tsp. Worcestershire sauce*
2 hard-cooked eggs	*½ tsp. sea salt*
	freshly ground black
½ cup minced parsley	*pepper to taste*
1½ tbsps. minced onion, optional	*½ stick melted sweet butter*
	1½ tbsps. mayonnaise

Mash livers with fork or put through meat grinder. Add remaining ingredients, blend until smooth. Refrigerate several hours to mellow. Serve with crisp crackers or melba rounds.

AFTERTHOUGHTS: Turkey liver pâté is terrific "brain food" because liver is rich in iron, phosphorus, and the B vitamins. Turkey liver can also be included in a delicious giblet gravy.

ROAST TURKEY EXTRAORDINAIRE

1 *cleaned, dressed turkey,*
  weighing about 18 lbs.
½ *cup minced onion*
½ *cup minced fresh dill*
6 *tbsps. minced fresh*
  parsley
3 *broken bay leaves*

2 *tsps. ground sage*
1 *clove garlic, optional*
1 *stick soft butter*
sea salt, black pepper to
  taste
candied kumquats,
  watercress

Clean turkey, washing outside and inside with water. Drain, pat dry. Rub inside cavity well with salt, pepper, onion, 2 tbsps. dill, 2 tbsps. parsley, bay leaves, and sage. Close neck, back openings by folding over skin; secure with skewers or stitching. Tie folded wings to back, legs to tail. Place bird on roasting rack in roasting pan, breast-side up. Rub skin with cut garlic and soft butter. Roast turkey uncovered in preheated 300° F. oven until tender. Allow 20 minutes per pound. During last 30 minutes of roasting time, cover skin with mixture of remaining dill, parsley, salt, and pepper. Turkey is done when leg meat feels soft when pressed with fingers and leg moves in thigh socket. Baste occasionally with pan drippings or butter. Let stand 10 to 15 minutes before carving. Garnish with candied kumquats and watercress. Serve hot or cold. Serves 12 to 14.

NOTE: Reserve giblets for making turkey pâté and turkey stock because Capricornian cooks are frugal and practical.

JEANE'S TURKEY STOCK

4 *cups water*
neck, giblets from 18-
lb. turkey
4 *bruised peppercorns*
1 *rib celery with leaves*

½ *carrot, chopped*
one small yellow onion,
peeled, cut in pieces
2 *lettuce leaves*
1 *lb. turkey liver*

Place all ingredients except turkey liver in a saucepan. Simmer 1 hour or until giblets are tender. Add turkey liver, simmer 5 minutes or until liver is barely tender. Remove turkey liver for pâté. Strain soup. Taste to correct seasonings. Serve as first course or use for making gravy.

WILLIAMSBURG INN OYSTERS

½ cup butter or
  margarine
½ cup chopped onion
⅓ cup chopped
  green pepper
1 clove garlic, mashed
½ cup unbleached flour
1½ tsps. paprika
½ tsp. salt
¼ tsp. freshly
  ground pepper
dash cayenne

1 tsp. Tabasco
1 tbsp. fresh lemon juice
1 tbsp. Angostura
  aromatic bitters
1 tsp. finely grated
  lemon rind
2 cups oyster liquor
3 cups well-drained oysters
½ cup coarsely
  crushed saltines

Melt butter in a skillet. Sauté onion, green pepper, and garlic until golden; stir in flour. Stir over heat until flour becomes golden. Stir in paprika, salt, pepper, cayenne, Tabasco, lemon juice, Angostura, lemon rind, and oyster liquor. Stir over low heat until sauce bubbles and thickens. Stir in oysters. Pour mixture into a buttered 1½-quart shallow baking pan. Sprinkle top with cracker crumbs. Bake uncovered in a preheated 400° F. oven for 20 to 25 minutes or until lightly browned and bubbly. Can also be spooned into individual 1-cup ramekins. Sprinkle tops with cracker crumbs and bake only 15 to 20 minutes. Serves 6.

AFTERTHOUGHTS: This celestial dish is terrific to serve with roast ham or fowl, particularly roast turkey in lieu of dressing. Makes a beautiful main dish offering for Sunday brunch or lunch, complete with a crisp garden salad of mixed greens. For a lovely dessert, lemon sherbet topped with crushed strawberries or raspberries.

CRANBERRY APPLE RELISH

2 cups fresh cranberries
2 red apples, cored but not
  pared
½ lemon, seeded

1 small onion
1 tsp. curry powder
1 cup sugar or honey

Rinse cranberries. Grind coarsely. Grind apples, lemon, and onion. Combine ground ingredients with curry powder and sugar or honey. Blend well. Let stand at room temperature for 1 hour. Cover, chill until ready to serve.

NOTE: Bright little cranberries, widely used by the Indians, are a fruit native to North America. Indians used them for a bright red dye for Indian clothes and poultices for wounds and infections. But their principal use was as an important ingredient in the Indian diet of pemmican cakes, made from a mixture of berries, dried meat, and fat. Pilgrim ladies found that cranberry provided certain medicinal benefits for the sick, particularly in instances of kidney problems. Used with meat or fowl, the tart little berry is a natural for those born under this cardinal sign!

SWEET POTATO PUFFS IN ORANGE SHELLS

3 oranges
6 medium sweet potatoes,
  cooked
1 stick sweet butter
½ tsp. sea salt

½ tsp. finely grated lemon
  rind
pinch cinnamon (or
  mace)
pinch cloves
pinch cardamon
2 tbsps. orange juice or
  cream
6 marshmallows

Cut oranges in half crosswise. Cut around inside of shells; scoop out pulp. Press pulp through sieve or ricer to extract juice. Set aside shells and juice. Mash potatoes; beat in butter, salt, lemon rind, cinnamon or mace, cloves, cardamon, and orange juice or cream. Pile sweet potato mixture into orange shells. Top each shell with marshmallow. Bake in preheated 350° F. oven 15 minutes or until lightly browned. Serves 6.

NOTE: Orange shells can be made in advance and frozen until ready to use.

JEANE DIXON'S FAVORITE DESSERT–BLUEBERRY * COMPOTE

1 cup blueberries,* fresh or
frozen, thawed
sprinkling of brown
sugar or a dollop of
strained clover honey
1 small ripe
but firm banana

1 ripe nectarine or
small peach, optional
cold milk or light cream,
depending upon my mood
ground cinnamon or
mace

Wash blueberries, drain on paper towels. Chill them well. Dust lightly with brown sugar or honey. Peel, slice banana over blueberries in bowl. Peel nectarine or peach; slice and mix with blueberries and banana. Top with cold milk or cream. If desired, dust fruit lightly with ground cinnamon or mace. Serve at once. Serves 1 to 2.

AFTERTHOUGHTS: Sometimes I add a dollop of sour cream or yogurt to the fruit to give it a sweet-sour effect. When I am very tired and not feeling up to par, I can make a whole meal out of blueberries and milk. My loving blueberries seems more than mere coincidence, especially since I have tremendous stars on each of my palms! That's why a gypsy told me I was a psychic when I was a child! The star-crossed blueberry with the 5-pointed star was treasured by ancient Indian tribes in America. According to Indian legend, during times of famine, the great spirit sent the "star berries" down from heaven to relieve the hunger of his children.

SCOTCH SHORTBREAD, FROSTED

For the shortbread:

1 cup butter
2 tsps. Angostura
   aromatic bitters

⅓ cup sugar
3½ cups unbleached flour

Have butter at room temperature. Mash butter, Angostura, and sugar until well blended and fluffy. Add flour; work into dough using hands. Cut dough into 4 pieces. Grease a cookie sheet. Place dough on cookie sheet. Press out evenly into four 7-inch rounds. Cut each round into 6 wedges with a knife. Bake in preheated 350° F. oven 20 to 25 minutes. Cookies will not brown. Cool shortbread on cookie sheets. Cut wedges again with a knife while cookies are still warm.

For the frosting:

2 cups sifted confectioners'
   sugar
grated rind of 1 orange

3 tbsps. lemon juice
1 tsp. Angostura aromatic
   bitters
1 tbsp. soft butter

Combine frosting ingredients; beat until smooth. Spread frosting on shortbread. Let dry at room temperature and then separate into wedges. Store in airtight container in a cool dry place. Makes 24 triangles.

GEWURZKUCHLEIN (GERMAN SPICE COOKIES)

3 eggs
1½ cups sugar
1 tsp. pure vanilla extract
3 cups unbleached flour
1½ tsps. ground cinnamon

¼ tsp. ground nutmeg
⅛ tsp. ground cloves
¾ tsp. baking powder
¼ tsp. sea salt

Beat eggs in large mixing bowl until soft. Gradually beat in sugar until mixture is pale and thick. Add vanilla extract. Sift flour with spices, baking powder, and salt. Add to egg mixture, blending well so dough is smooth but not sticky. Chill 1 hour. Sprinkle pastry board with confectioners' sugar. Roll out dough ½ inch thick. Make design with springerle roller or molds. Cut into squares as marked. Place cookies on greased baking sheets. Bake in preheated 325° F. oven 15 to 20 minutes or until edges are golden. Cool on wire racks. Store in airtight container. Can be stored several months. Makes 4 dozen cookies.

NOTE: A treasure of a cookie to make ahead and hold for a coffee break or a nifty offering when an unexpected guest comes to call.

KOURABIEDES (GREEK CHRISTMAS BUTTER COOKIES)

2 cups unmelted butter or
margarine, softened
½ cup confectioners'
sugar
2 egg yolks
2 tbsps. brandy
2 tsps. baking powder

1 can (4½ oz.) slivered
blanched almonds, finely
ground
5½ cups unbleached flour
whole cloves
confectioners' sugar

Cream butter in small bowl with sugar until light and fluffy
(mixture should resemble whipped cream). Blend in egg yolks,
brandy, and baking powder; mix well. Add ground almonds.
Gradually add flour; continue blending in mixer if possible or
work in remaining flour with hands or pastry blender. Turn
dough onto lightly floured board; knead until firm (about 10 to
15 minutes). Shape into walnut-size balls; stud each cookie with
a whole clove. Place on ungreased cookie sheets. Bake in preheated 350° F. oven 20 minutes or until nicely browned. Cool
slightly; dust generously with confectioners' sugar. Makes 9
dozen cookies.

NOTE: If desired, you may add 1 tsp. ground cloves to butter
mixture in place of whole cloves.

HOT LEMON TEA

1 quart freshly drawn cold
  water
1 tsp. lemon rind

6 tsps. loose tea or 6
  teabags
6 thin slices clove-studded
  lemon

Rinse teapot with hot water to warm it. Combine water and lemon rind in saucepan. Bring to full roiling boil. Pour over tea or tea bags. Let stand 3 to 5 minutes. Serve with clove-studded lemon slices. Serves 6.

NOTE: Tea is a toner for a weak stomach, good for steadying nerves, and a spectacular remedy for violent headaches and sickness occasioned by inebriation. Japanese mythology credits the origin of tea to the "White Buddha" Darma, an Indian high priest. During one of his meditations, contrary to his vows, the saintly man fell asleep. So great was his shame upon waking, he cut off his eyelids and threw them on the ground. The following day, to his amazement, he saw two small shrubs had sprouted from his eyelids. Curious, he tasted the flowers and immediately felt a divine elevation of mind; his disciples followed suit and so tea was given to the world!

JEANE'S SOUP

½ cup barley *
2 cups cold water
4 lbs. fresh tomatoes,
  peeled and diced
2 qts. hot water
1 large turnip (about 4
  cups), peeled and sliced
1 cup onion flakes
¼ cup celery flakes
2 bay leaves
2 tbsps. sea salt
1 tbsp. basil leaves
1½ tsps. instant minced
  garlic
1 tsp. honey

½ tsp. freshly ground
  black pepper
1 lb. eggplant, diced
4 cups diced cabbage
1 small cauliflower,
  cut into flowerets
2 cups corn off the cob
2 cups carrots, peeled
  and sliced
4 small zucchini,
  peeled and sliced
2 cups potatoes,
  peeled and diced
1 cup cut fresh snap beans
¼ cup parsley flakes

Soak barley in cold water for 12 hours. Put barley and barley water in large stock pot. Add tomatoes, hot water, turnip, onion and celery flakes, bay leaves, salt, 1½ tsps. of the basil leaves, minced garlic, honey, and black pepper. Cover, cook 1 hour. Add remaining ingredients except parsley; cook 45 to 60 minutes longer (or until vegetables are tender). Add remaining 1½ tsps. basil leaves and parsley. Taste to correct seasonings. Serve with long loaves of French or Italian bread, broken into hunks. Serves 12.

NOTE: Jeane's soup can also be made with meat: simmer 2 lbs. beef soup bones, 1½ lbs. neck meat, 2 lbs. knuckle bone, cracked, with 3 qts. water for 3 hours. Remove meat and bone from kettle. Discard bone. Strain stock. Then proceed as directed above, measuring soup stock to have 2½ qts. liquid, adding more water if necessary.

Barley,* an astrological ingredient in Jeane's soup, is a notable plant dominated by Saturn. Its virtues are many. It cools and cleanses the body and gives nourishment to people who are plagued with fevers, agues, and heats of the stomach.

NOODLE KUGEL WITH CHERRY * SAUCE

For the cherry * sauce:

*1 can (1 lb.) pitted sweet
　cherries*
2 tbsps. cornstarch
*1 tbsp. brown sugar
　or honey*
½ tsp. cinnamon

1 cup orange juice
1 tbsp. fresh lemon juice
*½ tsp. finely grated
　lemon rind*
1 tbsp. slivered almonds

Drain cherries; reserve syrup. Set aside. In saucepan, mix cornstarch with brown sugar (or honey) and cinnamon. Stir in orange juice, lemon juice, lemon rind, and reserved cherry juice. Boil ½ minute, stirring constantly. Add cherries and almonds. Heat, set aside.

For the kugel:

1 tbsp. sea salt
3 qts. boiling water
*6 oz. (about 4 cups)
　medium egg noodles*
*2 cups (1 lb.) creamed
　cottage cheese*
1 egg, beaten

*¼ cup firmly packed brown
　sugar or honey*
¼ tsp. cinnamon
dash sea salt
2 tbsps. slivered almonds
1 tbsp. butter

Add salt to rapidly boiling water. Gradually add noodles so water continues to boil. Cook uncovered, stirring occasionally, until tender. Drain in colander. Combine noodles with cottage cheese, egg, sugar or honey, cinnamon, salt, almonds, and butter. Turn into well-buttered 5½-cup ring mold. Bake in preheated 350° F. oven 40 minutes. Turn out onto serving plate and top with hot cherry sauce.

NOTE: Kugel is truly a Capricornian's delight! It provides needed calcium and the wonderful flavor of Venusian-dominated cherries.

SECOND DECAN: JANUARY 1 to JANUARY 9

Since I was born on January 5, Venus often makes me appear withdrawn and stresses my need for beauty, harmony, love, and cheerfulness. In reality, I love nothing more than entertaining my friends and family at intimate sit-down dinners at home. Typically, I plan a menu that is easy to prepare and serve. I adore beautiful flowers, exquisite china, crystal, silverware, and sparkling table linens. I enjoy a meal when it's beautifully served. I'm careful to select dinner guests who will enjoy the food as well as each other's company.

Since I'm almost a vegetarian, all milk products, especially mild cheeses, are very compatible with my sign and psyche. I like to prepare cannelloni (I use whatever I happen to have on hand to create the filling) or vegetarian spaghetti!

MARINATED MUSHROOMS

Cannelloni * or Vegetarian Spaghetti *

Italian Bread Sticks

Winter-Green Cabbage Salad with Dill-Lemon Dressing *

Cornucopia of Fruits and Assorted Cheeses

Coffee

- or -

MAJESTIC BROILED SHRIMP *

Stuffed Swedish Flank Steak *   Gravy

Snap Beans in Butter   Bouquet of Vegetables *

Knob Celery Salad *

Magnificent Muffins *   Butter

Red Raspberries * Capricorn *

Lemon Tea

CANNELLONI

For the pasta:

about 6 qts. water   6 oz. manicotti
salt

Bring salted water to roiling boil; add few manicotti at a time.
Cook 6 minutes or until pasta is barely tender. Plunge noodles
in cold water to rinse; drain on paper towels. Cook remaining
noodles until all the pasta has been cooked.

For the filling:

1 lb. ricotta cheese   1½ tbsps. chopped parsley or
1 cup cooked, drained   watercress
  chopped spinach   ⅛ tsp. nutmeg
1 hard-cooked egg, minced   ½ tsp. sea salt
about ½ cup freshly grated   freshly ground black
  Parmesan cheese   pepper to taste

Combine all ingredients; blend well. Stuff both ends of noodles
with filling. Set aside.

For the cheese sauce:

3 tbsps. butter	*sea salt, freshly ground*
2 tbsps. unbleached flour	*black pepper to taste*
2 cups milk	*6 tbsps. freshly grated*
	Parmesan cheese

Melt butter; blend in flour. Cook over low heat few minutes. Add milk gradually; add salt and pepper to taste with Parmesan cheese. Cook until smooth and thick, stirring. Grease a flat oven-proof baking dish with butter. Spoon a few tbsps. cheese sauce over the bottom of baking dish. Lay stuffed noodles carefully in baking dish. Spoon remaining sauce over all. Cover loosely with sheet of aluminum foil. Bake in preheated 350° F. oven about 20 minutes. Sprinkle remaining cheese over top of noodles. Bake 10 minutes longer or until sauce is nicely browned. Serves 6.

AFTERTHOUGHTS: Many fillings can be used. One of my favorites is made with leftover chopped cooked chicken, spinach, butter-fried bread crumbs, Parmesan cheese, Mozzarella cheese, cinnamon, or nutmeg. Others include beef, anise-flavored sweet Italian sausages, prosciutto ham, chopped mushrooms. Use a good, pungent marinara sauce!

VEGETARIAN SPAGHETTI

4 tbsps. margarine	*¼ tsp. freshly ground black*
2 tbsps. olive or vegetable	*pepper*
oil	*1 lb. fresh mushrooms*
1½ cups chopped onion	*1 good pinch cayenne*
1½ cups diced celery	*4 tbsps. chopped fresh*
1½ cups diced green pepper	*parsley*
½ cup diced carrot	*2 tsps. basil leaves,*
1 tbsp. minced garlic	*crumbled*
2½ lbs. fresh tomatoes,	*1 8-oz. pkg. Mozzarella*
peeled and mashed	*cheese, cubed*
1 bay leaf	*8 oz. hot cooked whole*
2 tsps. sea salt	*wheat spaghetti or soy*
1 tsp. oregano leaves,	*noodles*
crushed	*grated Parmesan cheese*

Heat 2 tbsps. margarine and oil in saucepan. Add onion, celery, green pepper, carrot, and garlic; sauté over moderate heat 10 minutes. Add tomatoes, bay leaf, salt, oregano, and black pepper. Cover, cook over moderate heat 1 hour, stirring occasionally. Meanwhile, rinse, pat dry, and slice mushrooms. Sprinkle mushrooms generously with cayenne. Sauté mushrooms separately in remaining margarine 5 minutes. Add mushrooms to sauce along with parsley and basil. Simmer 10 minutes longer. Stir in cheese. Spoon over cooked hot spaghetti. Sprinkle with grated Parmesan cheese. Serves 6.

WINTER-GREEN CABBAGE SALAD WITH DILL-LEMON DRESSING

*4 cups finely shredded
  cabbage
1 cup finely diced celery
3 tbsps. chopped fresh
  parsley
½ tsp. minced fresh chives*

*1½ tsps. dill weed
½ tsp. sea salt
freshly ground black
  pepper to taste
3 tsps. fresh lemon juice*

Combine all ingredients. Serve over shaved ice in individual glass salad bowls. Serves 8.

NOTE: Dill is said to avert the evil eye! Drink dill tea to overcome insomnia. The pungent herb was used by ancient Babylonian doctors. Injured knights of old placed burned dill seeds on their wounds to promote healing. Medieval gardeners raised dill for making love potions, the casting of spells, and charms against such spells. To avoid being hexed, people wore a bag of dried dill over the heart. Dill, being under Mercury's influence, is alleged to strengthen the brain and supposed to improve nerves, nails, hair, to quiet colicky babies, and to treat all digestive disorders. No one should be without it!

MAJESTIC BROILED SHRIMP

2 lbs. raw shrimp
¾ cup olive oil
1 garlic, halved
¼ cup chopped parsley

½ tsp. sea salt
2 tsps. Angostura aromatic
bitters

Remove shells from shrimp but do not remove tails. Combine all ingredients with shrimp. Marinate 1 hour. Put shrimp and marinade into a shallow oven-proof serving dish. Bake in preheated 450° F. oven 10 minutes or until shrimp are pink and lightly browned. Spear on toothpicks; serve hot. Or cook shrimp under a broiler or sauté in a skillet. Serves 6.

STUFFED SWEDISH FLANK STEAK

1 large flank steak
sea salt
1 tbsp. Angostura
aromatic bitters
½ cup pitted prunes,*
chopped
2 tart apples,* cored,
peeled, and chopped

3 slices bread, crumbled
1 tbsp. instant minced
onion
1 can (10½ oz.) condensed
beef broth
2 tbsps. butter
⅓ cup dry red wine

Sprinkle flank steak with salt. Brush steak with Angostura, only on inner surface. Mix prunes, apples, bread, and onion. Add ½ of the beef broth to stuffing. Mix well; spread on flank steak. Roll up jelly-roll fashion, starting at short side. Tie with string. Melt butter in a Dutch oven; brown steak on all sides. Add remaining broth to the Dutch oven; simmer closely covered 1½ to 2 hours (or until meat is tender). Place meat on a platter; cut into slices. If gravy is desired, pan juice may be skimmed of excess fat. Add ⅓ cup dry red wine and bring to a boil, scraping all particles from pan. Spoon pan juices over slices of meat. Garnish with radish roses, apple slices, and parsley. Serves 6.

AFTERTHOUGHTS: A terrific hearty meal for a blustery winter day. The sweet-sour dressing contains three foods ruled by Venus: apples, prunes, and wheat.

BOUQUET OF VEGETABLES

⅓ cup butter
⅓ cup unbleached flour
2 cups milk
2 cups grated Swiss cheese
2 tsps. Angostura
   aromatic bitters
sea salt

1 whole cauliflower
   boiling salted water
2 tbsps. butter
2 leeks, sliced
1 can (1 lb.) baby whole
   carrots, drained

Melt butter, stir in flour. Gradually stir in milk. Cook over low heat, stirring constantly, until sauce bubbles and thickens. Gradually beat in 1½ cups cheese. Stir in Angostura and salt to taste. Keep hot. Cook cauliflower whole in boiling salted water until tender but still firm. Melt butter, sauté leeks until soft and golden. Add carrots, stir. Cover, simmer gently until vegetables are hot. When ready to serve, drain cauliflower, place in center of a platter. Surround with leeks and carrots. Spoon sauce over cauliflower. Garnish with remaining cheese. Serves 6 to 8.

KNOB CELERY SALAD

1½ lbs. knob (root) celery
boiling salted water
4 tbsps. fine-grade olive oil
5 tbsps. vinegar
1 tsp. sea salt
½ tbsp. honey
1/16 tsp. freshly ground
black pepper

¼ cup beef broth, fresh
or canned
2 whole pickled beets,*
sliced
lettuce
snipped fresh parsley

Wash celery root; peel, cut in julienne pieces. Cover with boiling salted water. Boil until tender, about 5 minutes. Drain; let cool. Make a marinade using olive oil, vinegar, salt, honey, pepper, and beef broth; mix well, pour over cooked celery root. Marinate 1 hour in refrigerator. Drain; arrange celery on lettuce leaves with beet slices. Garnish with snipped parsley. Spoon marinade over salad. Serves 4.

AFTERTHOUGHT: My knob celery salad is an old family recipe. Celery root can be bought canned in fine gourmet shops or German grocery stores. Salad makes a delightful first course.

MAGNIFICENT MUFFINS

¼ cup butter or margarine
¼ cup honey
1 egg, well beaten
2 cups unbleached flour

4 tsps. baking powder
¼ tsp. sea salt
¾ cup milk

Cream butter; add honey and egg. Sift together flour, baking powder, and salt; add to creamed butter mixture alternately with milk. Bake in preheated 400° F. oven for 25 minutes. Serve at once with quince jelly.* Serves 6.

NOTE: Quince jelly is dominated by Saturn. Its juice, taken in small quantities, is a mild astringent stomachic medicine. Quince jelly is delightful spooned into baked apples.

RED RASPBERRIES * CAPRICORN

1 pkg. frozen red raspberries *	*1 tbsp. vanilla sugar or honey*
1 cup whipped heavy cream	*ground mace, optional*

Divide thawed raspberries, spooning berries into 2 tall sherbet glasses. Top with whipped cream sweetened with vanilla sugar or honey. Dust whipped cream lightly with ground mace. Serve at once. Serves 2.

NOTE: Vanilla sugar is easy to prepare: Cut a 1½-inch piece of vanilla bean; bury it in a canister of granulated sugar. Let sugar stand several days before using. The vanilla sugar perfumes and flavors the fruit, giving it a lovely, slightly aromatic flavor. Raspberries, a Venusian delight, strengthen the stomach and prevent sickness and retching.

THIRD DECAN: JANUARY 10 to JANUARY 19

To the qualities of Saturn add those of the planet Uranus and you are at your best in the kitchen. You're very creative and original—you can duplicate a great dish you had when you dined in a posh restaurant, only you make it better. Now you're ready for romance! You're anxious to cook that special meal to please the man in your life. In my case, my husband, Jimmy, just loves my buttermilk pancakes for Sunday night supper when just we two dine by the fireplace while Mike, my Magi-Cat, curls up by the fire.

At this time of the month, you're undoubtedly involved with some special project—completing a sculpture, making a new suit, or putting the finishing touches on a project for the P.T.A. Beware, because now you may get overtired. Don't neglect the other important areas in your life, namely your family, by just settling for whatever seems to satisfy their needs at that particular moment. Cabbage and kale should be an important part of your diet at this time to keep you in top form to ward off rheumatism and colds.

SUNDAY NIGHT SUPPER

Buttermilk Pancakes *   Cinnamon Apple Slices *

Grilled Canadian Bacon

Cranberry Wine Ice *   Milk

- or -

BACON-GRILLED HAMBURGERS

Baked Mushrooms and Barley *

Cardinal Beets in Orange Sauce *

Jeane's German Cabbage *

Tenth House Grapefruit Salad *

-or-

PETIT PUFFS, URANUS *   ASPARAGUS ROLLS *

Cream Cheese Rounds *

Orange Juice

Buttermilk

Chicken and Pimiento Tea Sandwiches *

Uranian Teatime Pound Cake *

Tea Concentrate *

BUTTERMILK PANCAKES

1 cup unbleached flour
½ tsp. baking soda
1½ tsps. baking powder
1 tbsp. honey
1 egg, beaten

2 tbsps. melted butter or
margarine, at room
temperature
⅔ cup buttermilk

Sift together flour, baking soda, baking powder, and sugar. Combine egg, butter or margarine, and buttermilk; add to dry ingredients, stirring just enough to dampen flour. The batter will be lumpy. Heat ungreased griddle over moderate flame. The griddle is hot enough when a few drops of cold water skid across the griddle. Pour about 3 tbsps. of batter for each cake onto hot griddle. Cook until cakes are nicely browned and bubbly. Flip to brown on other side. Serve at once with butter, strained honey, cinnamon apple rings, orange marmalade, or strawberry preserves and crisp bacon, Canadian bacon, sausage, or grilled ham steaks. Serves 3 or 4.

CINNAMON APPLE SLICES

3 large apples
3 tbsps. butter
¼ cup honey

½ tsp. ground cinnamon
3 tbsps. apple juice

Core, pare apples, cut into thin slices. Place in skillet with butter, sprinkle with honey and ground cinnamon. Cover, sauté over moderate heat 5 minutes. Turn apples slices once or twice. Add apple juice. Cover, simmer until tender. Serve hot or cold. Serves 6.

CRANBERRY WINE ICE

1 lb. fresh or frozen
cranberries
2 cups honey
2 cups orange juice

1 cup sauterne or
other white wine
1 egg white

Mix cranberries, honey, and orange juice in a saucepan. Cook at a slow boil for 5 minutes or until cranberries are very tender and mushy. It will take longer if the cranberries are frozen. Press cranberries through a sieve or food mill to make a purée. Stir in sauterne or other wine. Pour mixture into a freezer container. Freeze until half frozen. Scrape mixture into a bowl. Add unbeaten egg white and beat until smooth and fluffy. Pour back into freezer container and cover closely. Freeze until hard. Keeps well for several weeks in freezer if kept closely covered. Serves 8.

BAKED MUSHROOMS AND BARLEY *

1 lb. fresh mushrooms
½ cup margarine
1 cup coarsely chopped
onion
1½ cups pearl barley *

¼ cup chopped fresh parsley
2 cups beef broth
½ tsp. sea salt
⅛ tsp. freshly ground black
pepper

Rinse, pat dry and slice mushrooms. Melt half the margarine in large skillet. Add mushrooms and onion; sauté 2 minutes. Remove cooked vegetables to 1½-quart oven-proof casserole. Melt remaining margarine to skillet; add barley.* Cook, stir until barley is golden. Add barley with remaining ingredients to casserole; stir gently. Cover, bake in preheated 350° F. oven 50 to 60 minutes (or until barley is tender and liquid is absorbed). If barley appears dry, add more broth or water during cooking. Serve with hamburgers or steak. Serves 8.

NOTE: Barley, governed by Saturn, is delicious with mushrooms, ground lamb, onion, and tomatoes baked in a casserole. Freezes well, too, for the busy Capricornian cook.

CARDINAL BEETS * IN ORANGE SAUCE

*1-lb. can small whole
  beets,* drained*
*2 tbsps. butter or
  margarine*
1 tbsp. honey

*½ tsp. finely grated orange
  rind*
⅛ tsp. crushed cardamon
2 tbsps. fresh orange juice
2 tbsps. reserved beet juice

Combine ingredients, bring to boil, simmer 5 minutes. Serve piping hot. Great with sauerbraten, roast duck, or stuffed Swedish flank steak. Serves 6.

AFTERTHOUGHTS: The ruby-rooted plant, governed by Saturn, is economical and versatile. Pickle, boil, or sauté the root. In summer, when fresh beets are available, put tender leafy tops like greens in the pot with ham hock or ham bone; or wash greens carefully, crisp in refrigerator and toss in the salad bowl.

JEANE'S GERMAN CABBAGE

"The moon challengeth the dominion of the herb."
—Culpeper

4 cups shredded cabbage	2 tbsps. butter or
water	margarine
2 tsps. sea salt	2 tbsps. sour cream
hint of white pepper	1 tbsp. honey
1 tbsp. chopped onion	

Cover shredded cabbage with cold water, let stand 20 minutes to crispen cabbage. Drain, cook in rapidly boiling water with salt, pepper, and onion 5 minutes or until tender. Drain. Reheat; add butter, sour cream, and honey. Stir once before serving very hot. Serves 6.

AFTERTHOUGHTS: Can be made equally well with red cabbage. Delicious with grilled smoked pork chop and well-chilled homemade apple sauce.

TENTH HOUSE GRAPEFRUIT SALAD

1 large white grapefruit,	1 ripe but firm avocado,
sectioned	peeled, cut in thin slices
1 pink grapefruit, sectioned	few drops fresh lemon juice
1 persimmon, peeled, cut in	good bottled French or
thin slices	Italian dressing
	crisp, well-chilled chicory

Prepare fruit. Squeeze lemon on avocado slices to keep them from turning brown. Arrange fruits on salad plate alternating pink and white grapefruit, persimmon, and avocado to form a design. Drizzle fruit lightly with dressing. Garnish plate with chicory. Serves 6.

PETIT PUFFS, URANUS

½ cup butter or margarine
1 cup boiling water
½ tsp. sea salt

1 cup sifted unbleached
flour
4 eggs, unbeaten

Melt butter in boiling water in saucepan. Turn heat to low; add salt and flour, both at once. Stir briskly over low heat about 2 minutes until mixture leaves sides of pan in a smooth ball. Remove from heat. Add eggs, one at a time, beating well after each. Continue beating until mixture has a satinlike sheen. Drop by teaspoons, 1½ inches apart, on greased cookie sheets, shaping each into a mound that points up in center. Bake in preheated 400° F. oven about 20 minutes or until puffed high and golden brown. Cool on rack. Slice off tops and fill. Makes about 3 dozen puffs.

TUNA AND ALMOND FILLING

2 (6 oz.) cans light tuna
fish, drained

½ cup toasted, diced
almonds
⅔ cup mayonnaise

Drain and flake tuna. Mix with almonds and mayonnaise. Chill until ready to fill puffs.

ASPARAGUS ROLLS

20 to 22 slices bread
1 (10 oz.) pkg. frozen
asparagus spears
½ tsp. instant onion
bouillon

1 stick butter
1 tbsp. fresh lemon juice
½ tsp. paprika
green pepper

Trim crusts from bread. Flatten bread with rolling pin for easier handling. In the meantime cook asparagus according to package instructions, using instant onion bouillon instead of salt. Drain, cool. Spread bread with mixture of butter, lemon juice, and paprika. Place asparagus on each side of bread slice and roll firmly. Place seam side down. Cover with plastic and refrigerate until needed. Garnish with green pepper. Makes 20 to 22 sandwiches.

CREAM CHEESE ROUNDS

32 bread rounds, about 1½ inches in diameter
2 (3 oz.) pkgs. cream cheese
2 tsps. finely grated onion
2 dashes Tabasco sauce

1 envelope instant chicken-flavored broth mix
drained pimiento, cut in fancy shapes
watercress

Have cheese at room temperature. Combine with onion, Tabasco and broth mix. Spread on bread rounds. Garnish top with pimiento and watercress. Cover with plastic wrap and refrigerate. Makes 32 sandwiches.

CHICKEN AND PIMIENTO TEA SANDWICHES

2 (4¾ oz.) cans chicken spread
2 (4 oz.) jars whole pimientos, drained and minced
½ tsp. original Worcestershire sauce

½ tsp. lemon juice
3 dashes Tabasco sauce
1 (1 lb.) loaf unsliced bread
sprigs of fresh parsley

Mix chicken, pimiento, Worcestershire sauce, lemon, and Tabasco sauce. Chill. Slice crust from bottom of bread. Cut 8 thin slices. Remove crusts. Flatten with rolling pin for easier handling. Spread with chicken mixture. Roll up as for jelly roll. Wrap each in plastic. Chill until needed. Cut each roll into 6 slices. Garnish with fresh parsley. Makes 48 sandwiches.

URANIAN TEATIME POUND CAKE

2 tbsps. instant tea powder
1 tsp. ground cardamon
½ tsp. ground cloves
1 tbsp. finely grated orange
  rind

1½ cups milk
2 (1 lb. 1 oz.) pkgs. pound
  cake mix
4 eggs
confectioners' sugar

Mix tea, cardamon, cloves, and orange rind; blend carefully with milk so there are no lumps. Place cake mix in large bowl. Add 1 cup of the milk mixture. Blend until dry ingredients are moistened. Beat 1 minute at medium speed on electric mixer or 150 strokes by hand. Scrape bowl and beaters. Add eggs. Blend and beat for another minute. Add remaining milk. Blend and beat for another minute. Turn into a 10-inch greased and floured, or Teflon-lined, mold with hole in center—or a 9-inch or 10-inch slip bottom tube pan. Bake in preheated 300° F. oven for 1 hour and 20 minutes or until golden brown and top springs back when gently pressed with fingers. Cool in pan on rack for about 30 minutes. Remove from pan and continue cooling on rack. Dust top with confectioners' sugar. Serves 20.

AFTERTHOUGHTS: If smaller cake is desired: use 1 package mix, halving remaining ingredients. Pour into greased 9" × 5" × 3" loaf pan. Bake at 325° F. as suggested on the package.

TEA CONCENTRATE

1 qt. boiling water   *⅔ cup loose tea*
                                         boiling water

Pour 1 qt. boiling water over loose tea. Cover. Let stand 5 minutes. Stir and strain into a quart teapot or serving container. Use within 4 hours and keep at room temperature. Do not refrigerate. When ready to use, pour 2 tbsps. of concentrate in a cup and fill with boiling water. Makes 25 cups of hot tea.

NOTE: Tea concentrate is a fabulous boon to the solo cook who plans to prepare ahead and serve. For a delightful change of pace, use a spiced tea mix in lieu of loose tea.

AQUARIUS: JANUARY 20 to FEBRUARY 18

Read the Cookbook!

ALTHOUGH YOU ARE alternately turned on and off, up or down, you almost feel at times like you'd like to let it all pour out, just like your sign, the water-bearer.

Your most outstanding trait is your ability to remember. That's why you have never needed any formal cooking lessons. You learned to cook by watching your mother in the kitchen. Even though you have a memory like an elephant, you often leave out tiny details in a recipe. Better stick to the cookbooks for complicated cooking.

Despite your original ways, you have down-to-earth tastes and stick to tried and true foods such as steaks, chops, veal, and roasts. You're more likely to fill in with potatoes, vegetables (you like to grow your own) and seasonings. Although you eat as much protein as you like, avoid eating too much starch and sugar. Cholesterol can be a problem to you, especially in your late middle years.

You have a fetish for cleanliness and your kitchen shows it. You are a competent cook, often eager to try out new recipes or the latest kitchen gadget. During whimsical moments, you're keen on cooking "airy" foods: giant popovers, soufflés, and fluffy meringue pies.

Entertain on Saturdays and relax with Aries, Libra, and Gemini types.

FIRST DECAN: JANUARY 20 to JANUARY 29

Add onto the Aquarius/Uranus qualities the Saturn influences, and you become cautious and methodical in the kitchen, but sometimes secretive about the dinner you are whipping up.

You favor small intimate dinner parties for family or very close friends. You also favor old family recipes using simple, natural foods, with no artificial preservatives or flavorings added. Since you are practical and crave simple, carefully prepared foods, you keep the cost of food down. Due to the humane streak of some of you Aquarians, you are compelled to become vegetarians and forgo all flesh foods.

You're fond of the cabbage family, particularly red cabbage or cauliflower, plus wild rice and herbs (dried from your garden last summer).

———

LANCASHIRE HOT POT *

Shredded Green/Red Cabbage Salad   Applesauce

County Cork Soda Bread *

Skimmed Milk

-or-

BASQUE OMELET *

Ripe Olive Spinach Slaw *

Sweet Butter   Molasses Health Bread *

Cranberry Smash

LANCASHIRE HOT POT

2½ lbs. shoulder lamb chops,
cut ½ inch thick
2 lamb kidneys, skinned
and diced, optional
2 cups sliced onion
3 cups sliced potatoes

1½ cups hot beef broth
2 tbsps. original
Worcestershire sauce
1 tsp. sea salt
¼ cup unbleached flour

Trim fat from chops; place layer of chops in 3-quart casserole. Add kidneys. Top with half the onion; half the potato. Repeat layers of lamb, onion, and potato; end with potato. Combine broth, Worcestershire, and salt. Pour over lamb and vegetables. Cover, bake in preheated 325° F. oven 1½ hours or until lamb is tender. Remove casserole from oven. Increase oven temperature to 425° F. Carefully pour liquid from casserole into a measuring cup. Spoon off fat. Blend 2 tbsps. flour to each cup liquid in small saucepan. Cook, stir over low heat until thickened. Pour over meat and vegetables. Return to hot oven; bake uncovered 15 minutes longer or until potatoes are golden. Serves 6.

COUNTY CORK SODA BREAD

3 cups unbleached flour
1 cup wheat germ
3 tsps. baking powder
½ tsp. baking soda
1 tsp. sea salt

1 cup seedless raisins
1 tbsp. caraway seeds
1¾ cups buttermilk
¼ cup vegetable oil

Mix together flour, wheat germ, baking powder, soda, salt, raisins, and caraway seeds. Add buttermilk and oil. Stir just enough to moisten dry ingredients. Shape dough into two mounds on greased baking sheet. Bake in preheated 350° F. oven 50 minutes. Makes 2 loaves.

BASQUE OMELET

1 cup chopped onion
1 clove garlic, pressed
1 tbsp. salad oil
4 medium tomatoes
1 tsp. sea salt

1 tsp. dried basil
freshly ground black
  pepper to taste
1 California avocado
6 eggs
2 tbsps. margarine

Sauté onion and garlic in oil in saucepan over low heat. Peel, chop 3 tomatoes; add to onion mixture and cook, stirring occasionally, 5 minutes. Season with ½ tsp. salt, basil and pepper. Cover and keep warm. Slice remaining tomato. Halve, peel and slice avocado. Beat eggs with remaining salt in bowl until light and fluffy. Melt margarine in 9-inch skillet over low heat. Add egg mixture and cook until bottom is set. Spoon tomato sauce mixture over omelet and cook until desired. Top with tomato and avocado slices. Serve immediately. Serves 6.

RIPE OLIVE SPINACH SLAW

1⅔ cups canned pitted
   California ripe olives
4 cups shredded fresh
   spinach
1 thinly sliced carrot
¼ cup thinly sliced radishes
2 tbsps. thinly sliced green
   onion

1 cup cottage cheese
2 tbsps. salad oil
2 tbsps. cider vinegar
1 tsp. sea salt
¼ tsp. dry mustard
dash of Tabasco

Cut ripe olives into wedges and combine with spinach, carrot, radishes, and onion. Blend remaining ingredients and toss with spinach mixture. Serves 6.

NOTE: Salad makes a good one-dish meal made with sliced hard-cooked eggs, strips of American and Swiss cheese in lieu of cottage cheese. Serve with hot garlic-buttered whole wheat toast!

MOLASSES HEALTH BREAD

2¾ cups sifted unbleached
   flour
1½ tsps. baking powder
1 tsp. baking soda
1½ tsps. sea salt
1 tsp. cinnamon
½ tsp. mace
½ cup wheat germ
1 cup dark raisins, chopped

1½ tbsps. grated orange peel
1 egg, beaten
1 cup honey
1 container (8 oz.) plain
   yogurt
⅓ cup dark molasses
¼ cup orange juice
¼ cup melted margarine

Sift together flour, baking powder, baking soda, salt, cinnamon, and mace in large mixing bowl. Stir in wheat germ, raisins, and orange peel. In separate bowl, combine egg, honey, yogurt, molasses, and orange juice. Add to flour mixture, stir just until flour is dampened. Stir in melted margarine, barely mix until blended. Pour batter into well-greased 9″ × 5″ × 4″ loaf pan. Bake in preheated 350° F. oven 1 hour and 10 minutes or until cake tester inserted in center comes out dry. Cool 10 minutes; remove pan to wire rack; cool completely. Wrap in foil or plastic wrap and store overnight for easy slicing. Makes 1 loaf.

NOTE: Delicious served warm for dessert, topped with a scoop of pineapple sherbet!

SECOND DECAN: JANUARY 30 to FEBRUARY 8

Add on the qualities of Mercury and you become quick in the kitchen, inspired to create menus that are designed to be fixed ahead when you entertain the bridge club at home. You'll cook and play cards better if you dress casually for the occasion. Use leftovers and canned goods off the pantry shelf to avoid shopping in busy, crowded stores.

When you are planning social occasions for yourself, don't neglect your children.

––––––––

BRIDGE NIGHT CHOP SUEY *

Mandarin Oranges in Orange Gelatin *

Coffee   Tea

Honey Cake * or Hazelnut * Cake

- or -

TEENAGER'S SLUMBER PARTY FARE

Meat Loaf Pizza Supreme *

Green Salad *

Make-Your-Own Ice Cream Sundae *

Cranberry Punch *

Late Night Nibbles: Roast Pumpkin Seeds *

Mix 'n Munch Popcorn *

BRIDGE NIGHT CHOP SUEY

½ cup butter
5 cups cooked lean pork or
   chicken, thinly sliced
2 cups chopped onion
6 cups chopped celery
1 tbsp. sea salt
¼ tsp. freshly ground black
   pepper
3½ cups chicken broth
3 cans mixed Chinese
   vegetables

¼ cup cold water
¼ cup cornstarch
2 tsps. sugar
2 tbsps. leftover pork gravy
hot cooked rice
sliced green onion,
   hard-cooked eggs
   for garnishes, optional
soy sauce

Melt butter in skillet. Add meat and onion; cook 5 minutes.
Add celery, onion, salt, pepper, and chicken broth. Cover, cook
10 minutes. Add Chinese vegetables. Mix thoroughly, heat to
boiling point. Combine cold water, cornstarch, sugar, and gravy
to form smooth paste; add to meat mixture. Stir, cook 2
minutes. Spoon over hot cooked rice. Garnish with green
onion and sliced hard-cooked eggs. Pass soy sauce.
Serves 6.

NOTE: Terrific, fix-ahead answer to what to serve on bridge
night. Hardy enough for men, too, with little strain on the food
budget.

MANDARIN ORANGES IN ORANGE GELATIN

1 pkg. (3 oz.) orange-
  flavored gelatin
1 can (11 oz.) mandarin
  oranges
water

½ tsp. ground ginger
  or mace
crisp lettuce leaves
French dressing or
yogurt-mayonnaise,
  spiked with
  orange juice, optional

Place orange gelatin in mixing bowl. Drain mandarin oranges; reserve juice. Measure juice from oranges. Add enough water to juice to make 2 cups. Add ginger or mace to liquid. Heat until barely simmering; pour over gelatin, stirring to dissolve. Allow gelatin to cool; add oranges. Chill until well set. Serve on crisp lettuce leaves. Serve with French dressing or yogurt-mayonnaise dressing spiked with orange juice to taste. Serves 4 to 6.

HONEY CAKE

6 eggs
1 lb. honey
1½ cups sugar
1 cup cold coffee
1 tsp. grated lemon rind
1 cup fresh orange juice

5½ cups cake flour
3 tsps. baking powder
2 tsps. baking soda
¾ cup vegetable oil
  (unsaturated)

Beat eggs until thick and lemon-colored. Add honey, sugar, coffee, lemon rind, orange juice, cake flour (sifted together with baking powder and baking soda), and vegetable oil. Blend well, using electric mixer. Pour batter into a well-greased, deep, square cake pan. Bake in preheated 350° F. oven about 1¼ hours or until a toothpick inserted in cake comes out clean. Let stand 10 minutes before turning out on cake rack. Serves 15 to 20.

AFTERTHOUGHTS: A beautiful cake from an old family friend. It tastes even better the day after it is baked. Store in airtight box.

MEAT LOAF PIZZA SUPREME

1 lb. lean ground round
1 egg, lightly beaten
1 tsp. sea salt
¼ tsp. freshly ground black
pepper
2 cans (8 oz. each) tomato
sauce
½ cup Italian-flavored
bread crumbs
2 tbsps. grated Parmesan
cheese

2 tbsps. olive oil
4 tsps. basil leaves or
*savory ***
2 tsps. instant minced
onion
¼ tsp. garlic powder
5 or 6 thin slices
Mozzarella cheese

Mix together beef, egg, salt, and pepper. Pat into bottom and sides of a 9-inch pie plate. Set aside. Combine remaining ingredients except Mozzarella cheese; spoon into meat shell. Bake in preheated 375° F. oven 30 minutes. Top with Mozzarella cheese. Return to oven, bake 5 minutes longer or until cheese bubbles. Cool 5 minutes before cutting into pie-shaped wedges. Serves 6.

MAKE-YOUR-OWN ICE CREAM SUNDAE

Choice of different-flavored ice cream: chocolate, vanilla, strawberry.

Fruit toppings:	Homemade tutti-frutti: bananas, canned peaches, cherries, oranges, and a dash of sweetened lemon juice. Fix ahead and refrigerate until serving time. *Or* frozen, thawed strawberries mixed with frozen, thawed blueberries. *Or* whole peeled bananas, sliced over ice cream.
Syrups:	Bottled or homemade chocolate or butterscotch.
Trimmings:	Chopped nuts, malt powder, shaved chocolate, crushed peppermint. In other words, the works!
To assemble:	Prepare everything in advance, arranging all the toppings, syrups and trimmings on trays in refrigerator or on serving counter. Use paper plates, bowls; let everyone make his own sundae.

CRANBERRY PUNCH

*1 quart cranberry juice
    cocktail
1 pint orange juice
¾ cup fresh lemon juice*

*1 cup pineapple juice
⅓ cup strained honey
1 to 2 cups water*

Stir thoroughly. Serve over crushed ice or ice cubes. Serves 8 to 12.

ROAST PUMPKIN SEEDS

2 *cups pumpkin seeds*
1½ *tbsps. butter*

1¼ *tsps. sea salt*

Combine pumpkin seeds, butter, and salt. Mix well. Spread on cookie sheet. Roast in preheated 250° F. about 40 minutes or until browned and crisp, stirring often to brown evenly. Makes 2 cups.

MIX 'N MUNCH POPCORN

3 *qts. unsalted popped corn*
¼ *cup melted butter*
½ *can (3½ oz.) French-fried onions*

¼ *cup bacon bits or bacon-flavored bits*
sea salt to taste

Toss popped corn with melted butter. Stir in French-fried onions and bacon bits. Sprinkle with salt. Place mixture on a jelly-roll pan or baking sheet; heat in preheated 300° F. oven a few minutes. Serve hot. Serves 4 to 6.

THIRD DECAN: FEBRUARY 9 to FEBRUARY 18

Add on the qualities of Jupiter and your idealism and hospitable ways are fully realized as you plan lovely, offbeat vegetarian meals for family and friends. Since you now add the influence of Neptune, you tend to vacillate and daydream, thinking in terms of your spiritual needs rather than your gastronomic needs.

Your astrological food list includes: mushrooms,* peas,* asparagus,* dandelion greens,* endive,* oranges,* sage,* jasmine tea,* pine nuts,* and limes. Add more protein power by using cottage cheese or dairy products in luncheon or supper menus.

VEGETARIAN DINNER, AQUARIUS *

Giant Popovers * or Corn Bread

Endive Salad *

Fruit Tray

Sesame Cookies *   Jasmine Tea

- or -

SUPPER

Spinach and Cheese Pie

Winter Pear Banana Nut Salad *

Sweet Butter   Apricot Bread *

VEGETARIAN DINNER, AQUARIUS

2 cups cooked wild rice or
   brown rice
2 cups (16 oz.) drained
   green lima beans
1 cup cooked green peas *
1 cup sliced carrots *
½ cup fresh
   mushroom caps *

1 tsp. curry powder
3 cups water
2 chicken bouillon cubes
½ cup fresh cauliflower
   flowerets
1 cup fresh broccoli pieces
1 California avocado

Combine all ingredients except cauliflower, broccoli, and avocado in 2-quart saucepan. Bring to boil. Cook 35 minutes. Add cauliflower and broccoli. Cook 10 minutes longer. Spoon into heat-proof 2-quart casserole dish. Halve, peel, and slice avocado. Just before serving, lay over top of casserole dish. Serve with corn bread or popovers. Serves 6.

NOTE: Literally a medley of Aquarian foods! Nutsy sunflower seeds, pine nuts, * cheese, and eggs can add high-quality protein.

GIANT POPOVERS

6 eggs
¼ cup peanut oil
2 cups milk

1¾ cups unbleached flour
1½ tsps. sea salt

Combine eggs and peanut oil in large bowl; beat slightly. Gradually beat in milk, flour, and salt. Pour batter into 10 well-oiled custard cups. Place custard cups on baking sheet. Bake in preheated 375° F. oven 1 hour or until firm and brown. If desired, remove popovers from oven after 45 minutes, cut slits in the side of each to let steam escape, quickly return to oven for last 15 minutes. Makes 10.

ENDIVE SALAD

1 bunch Belgian endive
1½ tbsps. mayonnaise
1 tbsp. dairy sour cream or
   yogurt

¼ tsp. Dijon mustard
few drops fresh lemon juice
few drops Tabasco
sea salt, white pepper to
   taste
chopped fresh chives

Pull endive into separate leaves, rinse and dry on paper towels. Combine mayonnaise, sour cream, mustard, lemon juice, Tabasco, salt, and white pepper to taste; blend well. Spoon dressing over endive leaves on individual glass salad plates. Garnish with chives. Serves 4.

SESAME COOKIES

½ cup butter or margarine
1 cup sugar
1 egg
½ tsp. vanilla
¼ tsp. sea salt

2 cups sifted, unbleached
flour
¾ cup sesame seed, *
toasted

Cream butter and sugar thoroughly. Add egg, vanilla, and salt. Beat mixture until light and fluffy. Blend in flour and sesame seed.* Chill mixture 1 hour; shape into 2 rolls, 1½ inches in diameter. Wrap rolls in foil or plastic wrap; chill 4 hours or until firm. Slice ¼-inch-thick cookies from rolls; place on ungreased baking sheets. Bake in preheated 375° F. oven 8 to 10 minutes or until lightly browned on edges. Makes about 5 dozen cookies.

WINTER PEAR BANANA NUT SALAD

4 ripe winter pears,
washed and peeled
few drops lime or
lemon juice
2 large ripe bananas,
peeled and quartered

2 tbsps. finely chopped
peanuts or pine nuts *
about 2 tbsps. mayonnaise
few drops honey
watercress or romaine
lettuce

Core, halve pears. Squeeze lime or lemon juice on pears and bananas. Spread banana with mayonnaise mixed with honey; top with dusting of chopped nuts. Place pear halves and dusted banana pieces on salad plates. Garnish with watercress or romaine. Serves 8.

APRICOT BREAD

1 cup dried apricots
   grated rind of 1 lemon
⅓ cup orange juice
½ cup raw sugar or honey
3 cups whole wheat flour
1½ tsps. sea salt

½ tsp. soda
3 tsps. baking powder
1½ cups buttermilk
1 beaten egg
3 tbsps. melted margarine

Cut apricots in small pieces with scissors. Put apricots in saucepan with lemon rind, orange juice, sugar or honey. Cover, simmer 5 minutes. Combine dry ingredients; mix well. Mix together buttermilk, egg, and margarine. Beat in apricot mixture. Combine with flour. Bake in greased 8" × 11" pan in preheated 350° F. oven about 1 hour. Cool on wire rack. Serve with sweet butter. Makes 1 loaf.

PISCES: FEBRUARY 19 to MARCH 20

Fish Is the Dish!

LIKE YOUR SIGN Pisces, the fish, you make waves for all the world to see, but they are mere ripples compared to the depth of your emotions.

You have a unique talent for knowing what will happen before it happens. Like most Pisceans, you love to live and work near the water. As you might have guessed, fish is paramount in your diet. You could live off fish, attractively prepared and served in countless ways, but that does not make you alien to other foods, such as steak or baked potato.

You love to eat and are an inspired creative cook. You have a gift for giving the plainest of food a flair and a touch of artistry with unusual and exotic foods. You like to entertain on Thursdays, especially at small dinner parties for close friends and family. You are an outstanding host or hostess, but not the best homemaker in the world. You are bored with the tedium of everyday cooking. You love romantic places, selecting restaurants that serve excellent fare in quiet, relaxed surroundings. You're happiest around young people, particularly if they are Virgo, Cancer, and Scorpio types.

FIRST DECAN: FEBRUARY 19 to FEBRUARY 28

Since you're influenced mainly by Neptune and Jupiter, you are an inspired cook and look on food as entertainment as much as sustenance for the body. One of your happiest ways to entertain during cold wintery days is over the chafing dish. Gather up anything, from choice beef to good cheese, and the party is on! A tossed crisp green salad or dessert tray of fruits and cake is the perfect way to include your astrological foods: pine nuts,* asparagus,* chestnuts,* chervil,* currants,* endive,* limes,* and oranges.

One word of caution, though: be careful not to drink too much. (Pisceans have a low tolerance for drugs or alcohol.)

BEEF FONDUE *

Red Sauce *   Mustard Sauce *   Apricot Sauce *

Peas * with Lemon Mint Sauce *

Endive * Salad with Lime Dressing

Assorted Bread Tray: Water Biscuits,

Crusty Italian Bread

Orange Cake or Cantaloupe Cup *

Ginseng Tea *

BEEF FONDUE

2 lbs. fillet of beef, cut into
¾-inch cubes
½ cup butter

⅔ cup shortening, melted
prepared sauces (red
sauce, mustard sauce,
apricot sauce)

Arrange meat on large platter or individual plates. Heat butter in top of double boiler over boiling water to clarify it. Pour off and discard top milky layer; retain clarified butter. Combine clarified butter and shortening in fondue pot. Heat to 400° F., using deep-fat thermometer. Bring fondue pot to the table, place it over its heat source. Put sauces in individual dishes at each place. Let each person spear his own meat on a fondue fork and cook in the hot oil to suit himself. Allow 20 seconds for rare. To keep oil hot enough, only two people at a time should brown the meat. An electric fondue pot eliminates this concern. Remove cooked meat from fondue fork to the plate. Dip cooked meat in one or more of the sauces before eating. Serves 4 to 6.

RED SAUCE

½ cup seafood cocktail
sauce
1 tsp. fresh lime * or lemon
juice

¼ tsp. onion powder
½ cup dairy sour cream

Combine cocktail sauce, lime or lemon juice, and onion powder. Fold in sour cream. Chill to blend flavors. Serve with meat. Makes 1 cup.

MUSTARD SAUCE

¾ tsp. dry mustard
¾ tsp. Worcestershire sauce

¼ tsp. garlic salt
1 cup sour cream

Combine mustard, Worcestershire, and garlic salt. Fold in sour cream. Chill to blend flavors. Serve with meat. Makes 1 cup.

APRICOT SAUCE

1 jar (12 oz.) apricot
 preserves
4 tsps. white vinegar

¾ tsp. ground mace
⅛ tsp. salt

Combine all ingredients in small saucepan. Bring to boil; simmer, stirring constantly, about 2 minutes or until slightly thickened. Makes about 1½ cups.

PEAS * WITH LEMON MINT SAUCE

3 cups fresh, shelled peas
  (or frozen peas)
3 tbsps. melted margarine
1 tbsp. fresh lemon juice
¼ tsp. finely grated
  lemon rind

2 tbsps. chopped fresh mint
  or dried mint flakes
sea salt, white pepper
  to taste

Cook peas in small amount of water until barely tender. Add remaining ingredients. Season to taste. Serves 6.

NOTE: Mint, the Venusian herb, is the symbol of hospitality and wisdom. "The very smell of it reanimates the spirit," Pliny wrote. Mint was once a nymph, called Mentha, who attracted the roving eye of Pluto. His wife, in a jealous fury, knocked Mentha down, almost trampling her to death before Pluto appeared on the scene and turned her into this delightful herb!

CANTALOUPE CUP

2 cantaloupes
2 cups dry-packed
  blueberries, thawed

1 cup orange yogurt or
  strained honey or
  coconut

Cut cantaloupes in half. Fill with blueberries. Top with dollop of orange yogurt or honey to taste, or flaked coconut. Serves 4 to 6.

AFTERTHOUGHTS: If desired, cut melons in small pieces and peel. Marinate in orange *-lime *-honey sauce. Serve in sherbet glasses topped with coconut.

GINSENG TEA

1 oz. ginseng root   *few slices ginger root*
6 cups water

Boil ginseng root in water; add ginger root for flavor as desired. Boil ginseng in water down to 3 cups. Serve alone or with milk. Serves 3.

NOTE: Ginseng tea is available in root or powdered form. It is thought to prolong life! Ancient Chinese medicine is rooted in the very soil that gave rise to Chinese civilization. Emperor Shen-nung (said to have lived from 3737 to 2697 B.C.) is credited with founding agriculture and performed the first experiments with herbal remedies. *Panax ginseng* is native to China, Korea, and Siberia. Its North American counterpart, *Panax quinquefolium* (five-fingered root), is also believed to have medicinal value and appears in the medicinal folklore of many American Indian tribes. The root is creamy or white and resembles a parsnip, with rootlets branching off to suggest the shape of the human body. Ancient Oriental astrologers linked ginseng to the man-figure of Orion and believed that the astral influences of Orion could determine the potency of ginseng in every person.

SECOND DECAN: MARCH 1 to MARCH 10

Add the influence of the moon, and you are highly imaginative in the kitchen, especially when it comes to adapting menus that will please family and friends. Since you are sensitive to their reactions, choose foods carefully, cook and present them attractively.

Your lunar astrological foods can challenge you to create interesting salads (watercress,* turnips *—eat them raw—cucumbers,* lettuce,* and pumpkins *) to include with fish or meat.

PISCEAN ROCK LOBSTER AND BEAN SALAD *

Chived Carrots *   Broccoli

Cucumber Melon Salad *   Bran Muffins *

Limed Avocado Ice Cream *

- or -

FISH DINNER ON A PLANK *

Cucumber Melon Salad *

Salt Sticks

Pumpkin Tarts

PISCEAN ROCK LOBSTER AND BEAN SALAD

8 (2 oz. each) South
African rock lobster tails,
frozen
1 can (1 lb. 4 oz.) chick-
peas, drained
1 can (15½ oz.) kidney
beans, drained
1 can (7 oz.) sweet red
pimientos, drained,
chopped

2 medium-sized dill pickles,
diced
1 green pepper, chopped
½ cup scallions, sliced
shredded green cabbage
or watercress
⅔ cup dairy sour cream
⅔ cup mayonnaise
2 tbsps. prepared mustard
3 tbsps. catsup

Drop lobster tails into boiling salted water. When water reboils, boil for 3 minutes. Drain immediately, drench with cold water. Remove lower skin, pull out lobster meat in one piece. Cut each tail into halves lengthwise. Combine chick-peas, kidney beans, celery, pimientos, pickles, pepper, and scallions. Chill thoroughly. Combine sauce ingredients. For each serving, place 1 cup of bean mixture and 2 halves of lobster meat on top of shredded cabbage or watercress in serving dish. Top with sauce. Serves 8.

CHIVED CARROTS

6 medium-sized carrots
¼ cup margarine
¼ tsp. sea salt

⅛ tsp. white pepper
1 tbsp. snipped fresh chives

Scrub, chop carrots. Cook until slightly tender. Add margarine, salt, pepper, and chives. Serve piping hot. Serves 6.

CUCUMBER * MELON * SALAD

½ lb. peeled, sliced
   cucumbers *
2 cups peeled, diced
   cantaloupes *
¼ cup French dressing
   (homemade or bottled)
few drops fresh lemon
   or lime juice

¼ tsp. finely grated
   lemon rind
1 tbsp. chopped fresh dill
   or 1 tsp. dill seed
crisp cleaned watercress *
   or lettuce

Combine cucumber, cantaloupe, and remaining ingredients except watercress or lettuce. Serve on watercress or lettuce as first course or with meat or fish course. Serves 4.

HOMEMADE FRENCH DRESSING

3 tbsps. vegetable oil
3 tbsps. lemon juice or
   wine vinegar
sea salt, pepper to taste
   dash of soy sauce

choice of herbs: oregano,
   basil, thyme, curry
   powder, caraway, dill, or
   sesame seeds

Put all ingredients in wide-mouth screwtop jar. Shake well before using.

BRAN MUFFINS

¼ cup margarine
¼ cup light molasses
1 egg
1 cup whole bran
¾ cup milk
1 cup sifted unbleached
   flour

2½ tsps. baking powder
½ tsp. sea salt
½ cup finely chopped dates
   or currants

Blend together margarine and molasses. Add egg; beat well. Stir in bran and milk; let stand until moisture is absorbed. Sift together flour, baking powder, and salt. Add flour mixture to molasses mixture with dates or currants. Stir only until blended. Fill greased muffin cups ⅔ full. Bake in preheated 350° F. oven 30 minutes. Makes 12 small muffins.

NOTE: Delightful, too, for breakfast or brunch with fluffy scrambled eggs, or terrific with Boston brown bean bake for vegetarian nutritious dinner!

LIMED AVOCADO ICE CREAM

2 soft California avocados,
   peeled and pitted
¼ cup fresh lime juice

½ cup honey
½ pint whipping cream

Mash avocado, lime juice, and honey with electric mixer or blender. Spoon into freezer tray. Freeze until almost firm. Stir once with spoon, refreeze. Makes about 1 quart.

AFTERTHOUGHTS: No wonder Pisceans love avocados! Avocados contain huge amounts of vitamins A and E, and a good supply of vitamins B and C. They are rich in iron, too.

FISH DINNER ON A PLANK

*1 3- to 4-lb. cleaned,
dressed whole sea bass or
red snapper
lemon juice or lemon-
pepper seasoning
1 can (6 oz.) crabmeat
⅓ cup cream of mushroom
soup (canned, undiluted)
4 strips lean bacon
2 cups seasoned, hot
cooked rice or small
whole red potatoes,
cooked in the jacket*

*seasoned, hot cooked
vegetables: whole baby
carrots, turnips (cut in
small round balls),
asparagus bundles
parsley sprigs or watercress*

Wash and dry fish thoroughly. Sprinkle inside cavity with lemon or lemon-pepper seasoning. Mix crabmeat with mushroom soup. Put 2 strips bacon on preheated oiled plank or large greased bake-and-serve platter. Lay fish on plank or platter. Stuff cavity with crabmeat mixture. Secure edges loosely with foil. Put remaining bacon on top. Bake in preheated 350° F. oven 45 minutes or until fish flakes easily with fork. Arrange rice or potatoes and vegetables around fish. Garnish with parsley or watercress. Serve immediately. Serves 6.

THIRD DECAN: MARCH 11 to MARCH 20

Add on the influences of Mars, and you are impulsive and energetic in the kitchen! Due to your contrasting moods, it's better to stick to tried and true recipes. Opt for a wonderful piece of beautiful broiled fish—terrific for dieters—or a hearty, he-man lamb stew and rice. Follow your Martian influences and create a hot herbed sauce for the fish using your pick from your astrological foods: cayenne,* garlic,* parsley,* rosemary,* basil,* onion,* chives,* or mustard.* Cool it down with a delicious, old-fashioned rice pudding.

LAMB STEW *

Lettuce-Parslied * Salad

Baked Apples in Foil *

- or -

LEMON-BROILED SWORDFISH

Herbed Sauce (mayonnaise spiked with parsley,
chives, * and horseradish *)

Brussels Sprouts

Raisin Rice Pudding Bake *

LAMB STEW

1½ lbs. lean lamb shoulder
1½ tsps. sea salt
¼ tsp. freshly ground black
  pepper
1 clove pressed garlic *
1 tsp. vegetable oil
2 cups beef broth
⅓ cup dry white wine
½ cup chopped green
  onions with tops

2 cups diagonally sliced
  carrots
1½ cups cubed turnips
¼ tsp. basil
½ tsp. rosemary
1 bay leaf
1 tbsp. cornstarch
2 cups hot cooked rice

Season lamb with salt, pepper, and garlic. Brown in oil. Add broth, wine, vegetables and seasonings. Bring to a boil, cover, reduce heat. Simmer 1 hour. Mix 2 tbsps. water into cornstarch. Stir into stew. Cook 2 minutes longer, stirring. Remove bay leaf. Serve over beds of fluffy rice. Serves 6.

BAKED APPLES IN FOIL

4 *baking apples*
2 *tbsps. quince jelly*
½ *lemon*
½ *tsp. cinnamon*
¼ *tsp. nutmeg*

2 *tbsps. butter or*
   margarine
heavy cream, plain or
   whipped

Core, peel apples halfway down from stem end of each apple. Place each apple in center of a square of aluminum foil. Fill center of each apple with quince jelly, few drops lemon juice, cinnamon, nutmeg, and butter or margarine. Bring foil over apples and crumple ends of foil together but not tightly. Some steam should escape as apples roast. Place foil-wrapped apples in shallow baking pan. Bake in preheated 375° F. oven 45 minutes. Turn back foil 10 minutes before apples are done. Baste apples several times with jelly-lemon mixture during remaining cooking time. Serve warm, plain or with heavy cream. Serves 4.

RAISIN RICE PUDDING BAKE

1 *pkg. vanilla pudding*
2½ *cups milk*

2 *cups cooked rice*
½ *cup raisins*

Empty contents of package into saucepan. Gradually add milk, stir to keep mixture smooth. Cook over medium heat, stir constantly until pudding comes to a boil. Stir in remaining ingredients; pour into greased baking dish. Bake in preheated 350° F. oven 25 minutes or until pudding begins to bubble. Serve hot, or chill well and serve. Serves 6 to 8.

The year's at the spring
And day's at the morn;
Morning's at seven;
The hillside's dew-pearled;
The lark's on the wing;
The snail's on the thorn:
God's in his heaven—
All's right with the world!

—ROBERT BROWNING

INDEX